W9-BRW-919

Set *for* Life

Set *for* Life

FINANCIAL PEACE
FOR PEOPLE OVER 50

Bambi Holzer

with

Elaine Floyd

John Wiley & Sons, Inc.

New York • Chichester • Weinheim • Brisbane • Singapore • Toronto

This book is printed on acid-free paper. ∞

Copyright © 2000 by Bambi Holzer. All rights reserved.

Published by John Wiley & Sons, Inc.

Published simultaneously in Canada.

No part of this publication may be reproduced, stored in a retrieval system or transmitted in any form or by any means, electronic, mechanical, photocopying, recording, scanning or otherwise, except as permitted under Sections 107 or 108 of the 1976 United States Copyright Act, without either the prior written permission of the Publisher, or authorization through payment of the appropriate per-copy fee to the Copyright Clearance Center, 222 Rosewood Drive, Danvers, MA 01923, (978) 750-8400, fax (978) 750-4744. Requests to the Publisher for permission should be addressed to the Permissions Department, John Wiley & Sons, Inc., 605 Third Avenue, New York, NY 10158-0012, (212) 850-6011, fax (212) 850-6008, E-Mail: PERMREQ @ WILEY.COM.

This publication is designed to provide accurate and authoritative information in regard to the subject matter covered. It is sold with the understanding that the publisher is not engaged in rendering professional services. If professional advice or other expert assistance is required, the services of a competent professional person should be sought.

Library of Congress Cataloging-in-Publication Data:
Holzer, Bambi.
    Set for life : a retirement planning guide for people over 50 /
Bambi Holzer with Elaine Floyd.
        p.   cm.
    Includes index.
    ISBN 0-471-32114-1 (cl. : alk. paper)
    1. Aged—Finance, Personal.   2. Retirement—United States—
Planning.   3. Retirement income—United States—Planning.
4. Estate planning—United States.   I. Floyd, Elaine, 1946–   .
II. Title.
HG179.H5952   2000
332.024'01—dc21   99-18530

Printed in the United States of America
10 9 8 7 6 5 4 3 2 1

This book is dedicated to my mother, Estelle Holzer.

Contents

PART I—PLANNING

Where Do You Stand Today?

- Financial situation—What do you have and where is it?
- Knowledge base—How much do you know and how much do you need to know?
- Preparedness—What have you done and what do you need to do?

How and Where Do You Want to Live?

- A look at creative aging
- What will you be doing with your time?
- Where will you live?

How Much Will It Cost to Live?

- Looking toward the future—How will your expenses change?
- What to do about inflation
- Expense categories—What is likely to change in the future?
- Is your spending plan reasonable?

Foreword

Bambi Holzer is one of PaineWebber's most respected financial advisors who truly cares about her clients—not just the rate of return on their portfolios but how their investment program can help them live better lives. To Bambi, investing is not just about the economy and the markets (as Chief Investment Officer for Equities at Mitchell Hutchins, that's my job). It's about helping people understand what's important in life and putting their money to work so they can achieve their goals. Bambi gets inside the minds and hearts of her clients and helps them plan for a secure future.

In this, her second book on retirement planning, she presents a wealth of information that anyone over 50 can use. And it doesn't matter whether the reader is contemplating retirement, is already retired, or plans never to retire. The financial considerations presented here affect nearly everybody—working or not—as they grow older and prepare for a long and comfortable life. Financial facts are blended with lifestyle issues because that's how most people approach money—in the context of their lives. At the same time, the chapters on investing are as professional as they can be, reflecting Bambi's keen understanding of investments and how she guides clients in putting together a portfolio that meets their financial objectives.

One of the best aspects of this book is its clear, fluid, easy-to-read writing style. Bambi and her co-author, Elaine Floyd, explain complicated financial concepts in terms that are understandable to the average reader, blending humor and substance in a way that makes the book both fun and informative. Even people who have avoided financial books in the belief that they are all dry, boring, and incomprehensible will be pleasantly surprised by this book. Although packed with useful information, it's still a quick read. Respectful of the reader's time, the authors invite the reader to skip over any parts that are either too basic or don't apply to his or her current situation.

I value my association with Bambi and have great respect for her ability to bring financial information to people with varying levels of investing experience. I wish her great success on her second book.

Mark Tincher
Chief Investment Officer, Equities
Mitchell Hutchins, the investment
management subsidiary of PaineWebber, Inc.

Preface

H ow can I be sure I'll have enough money to last the rest of my life?"

That's always the first question that comes up when I ask people over 50 to tell me about their financial concerns. Nobody wants to work forever. Nobody wants to become dependent on relatives or the government in their old age. Everybody wants to live a long, happy life and *not ever have to worry about money.*

It's not as if people suddenly become mercenary and materialistic when they turn 50. In fact, the opposite is true. It's because people *don't* want to have to think about money that they are so concerned about it when they reach a certain age. So my advice is always the same: Spend a little time up front putting all of the investment and financial planning pieces in place, and then go off and enjoy yourself.

My first book, *Retire Rich: The Baby Boomer's Guide to a Secure Future,* addressed the concerns of people in their 30s, 40s, and early 50s. People who are in their peak earning years and who have several decades to go before they retire are primarily concerned about building a nest egg for the future. They want to know how much they need to save while they are still working and how to invest those savings for maximum growth.

People over 50, on the other hand, are more concerned about keeping what they have. They're not necessarily trying to get rich. They just want to have a comfortable lifestyle and make their money last as long as they do. So while my first book focused on building wealth, this book focuses on building *and preserving* wealth, so people over 50 can live their lives in comfort and security, without having to worry about money.

In my 18-year career as an investment executive, I have worked with many hundreds of people in their 50s, 60s, 70s, and 80s. Some of my clients have more money than they could ever spend in a lifetime, while others need to be very careful about how they spend, save, and invest in order to make their money last. Some of my clients sail through life, enjoying happy marriages and an abundance of grandchildren, while others are forced to deal with the pain of widowhood or divorce. Some of my clients are very savvy about investing and financial planning, while others depend on me to guide them each step of the way. What all of my clients have in common is the singular goal that is most often stated this way: "I/we want to be set for life."

I realize that financial matters are not always the most fun things to deal with, so I applaud you for picking up this book and being willing to spend a few hours concentrating on the financial issues that can make a difference in your life. Once you have your financial plan in place and know what you have to do to stay financially secure, you can focus on the really important things in life, like family, friends, and making a contribution to the world.

Wishing you much success and happiness in life.

Bambi Holzer
Los Angeles, California
November, 1999

Acknowledgments

This book was made possible by the expertise and tireless efforts of many people:

The professionals who reviewed the manuscript for technical accuracy: Steve Krell, CPA, partner with Alder, Green, and Hasson in Los Angeles; Mark Hess, attorney with Jeffer, Mangels, Butler, and Marmaro in Los Angeles; Pat Byrnes, president of Actuarial Consultants Incorporated in Torrance, California; Andy Katzenstein, attorney with Katten, Muchin & Zavis in Los Angeles; Pam Garvin, attorney at law in Los Angeles; and Marvin Cohen, president of Progressive Planning Inc., in Sherman Oaks, California.

My colleagues at PaineWebber: Margo Allen, Director of Retirement Services; Donna Peterman, Mary McPartland, and Christene Kauffman in Corporate Communications; Gary Stegland, Sandy Stern, and Even Gordan in Compliance; Mike Davis, Scott Flanigan, Barry Harberson, Bonnie Freer, Bonnie Samuels, Frank Epinger, Howard Kern, Tod Winkler, Jenny Brearton, Michael Lutz, and Sharon Shelton in Los Angeles.

The publishers and agents who made the book happen and brought it to the public eye: Myles Thompson, Debby Englander, and Peter Knapp at John Wiley & Sons; publicist Dick Wolfe with Communications/Marketing Action, Inc. in New York; and agent Craig Foster with Robert Lewis Rosen Associates, Ltd., in New York.

My wonderfully supportive family: My aunt and uncle, Jean and Ralph Heller; my sister Audrey, her husband E. Leonard Rubin, and their daughters Margot and Bette; my children Danny Schatz, Alison and Steve Daniels, and darling Madison; and my fabulous husband Charles, who has the patience of a saint and is always by my side.

PART ONE

Planning

CHAPTER ONE

Where Do You Stand Today?

Knowledge is the antidote to fear.

—Ralph Waldo Emerson

Ask people over the age of 50 what their financial concerns are and you'll hear answers ranging from "When can I afford to retire?" to "How do I make sure my spouse is taken care of after I die?" People over 50 represent a broad range of circumstances: Some are still working, others are happily retired. Some have plenty of money, others are just scraping by. Some are financially savvy, others are totally clueless about investments and financial planning. But whether you are 55 and working or 95 and living off your investments, you have one thing in common with everyone else enjoying the last third of life: You want to make sure your money will last at least as long as you do. You want to be set for life.

You're probably more realistic about money today than you were when you were younger. If you're not already a millionaire, you no longer have dreams of becoming one. If you have managed to accumulate a sizable nest egg, you want to make sure you don't lose what you have. You no longer see money as something to chase but rather a medium of exchange that will allow you to live the rest of your life in comfort—as long as you have enough of it.

If you've managed to keep your financial life fairly simple up to now, you may be finding that money matters get much more complex as you get older. Keeping up with Social Security and Medicare is challenging enough, but if you're also managing an investment portfolio, taking individual retirement account (IRA) distributions when you're supposed to, making sure your family will be taken care of after your death, all while saving as much on your income tax as you can, you know how challenging and time-consuming personal financial management can be. But the alternative is worse. By not staying on top of financial matters, you could find yourself in desperate circumstances just when you should be kicking back and enjoying life.

In this book you will read about the various parts of your financial life that all work together to provide the ultimate goal of financial security. And these parts really do all work together. You can't manage an investment portfolio without thinking about taxes. You can't draft a will that conflicts with IRA beneficiary designations. You can't make decisions about when to start collecting Social Security benefits without considering other income from employment. So if you've managed to get this far without understanding the basics of personal finance, you have some catching up to do. And if you've been pretty good about learning as you go along—brushing up on 401(k) plans and investments while you were saving for retirement, for example—you have a bunch of new stuff to learn as you get older. Social Security rules. IRA distribution rules. Estate planning rules. Long-term care insurance options. Of course, you can hire professional advisors to guide you. But for your own peace of mind, you'll want to have a basic understanding of these matters so you can guide the advisors and be in control of your finances.

HOW THIS BOOK IS DIFFERENT

This book is different from other retirement planning books in several ways. It takes a new approach that reflects today's lifestyles and trends, addressing the various financial topics as they relate to the way people live today. After all, what good is money if it doesn't make your life better in some way?

Changing Ideas About Retirement

The classic notion of retirement—where you'd spend thirty or forty years working for the same company, retire at age 65, putter around the house for another seven-point-five years and then die—has been replaced with a newer, healthier concept of "retirement." Instead of age 65 marking the end of work and the beginning of play (or doing nothing at all), people are transitioning to "retirement" by cutting back their hours, shifting from corporate employee to part-time or freelance worker, and generally designing creative careers that give meaning and satisfaction to their lives. In many cases this new concept of retirement is not defined by age at all. Some people find themselves totally burned out at 40; after transitioning to a more fulfilling (and often lower-paying) career, they figure they'll work forever, and happily so. Others are retiring from their primary careers at the traditional age of 60 or 65 and finding a different form of paid employment that brings far more satisfaction than their long-held jobs ever did. They too plan to work forever, either because they like the work or need the money, or both. Still others receive their last paycheck, throw themselves into philanthropy or volunteerism, and end up working harder than they ever did when they were "working." So when we talk about retirement, we are not necessarily talking about that period of your life when you are not working anymore. Instead, we are talking about the last third to half of your life, which may be characterized by work (for pay or not) or play or all of the above.

Family Planning

Our concept of family planning is not what you think. Rather it is a strategy that incorporates the extended family into the financial planning process to meet the needs of the sandwich generation that is caring for 85-year-old parents at the same

time their 30-year-old children are moving back home. As much
as you may want to be financially independent and see your parents and children be the same, in some families it just doesn't
work that way. They need you. And you may need them someday. So rather than deny this interdependence among generations, it's better to accept it and plan for it. Without necessarily
commingling funds or transferring assets to family members
(unless it makes sense to do so, either for estate planning or tax
reasons), you may want to consider your parents' and/or children's financial circumstances when doing your own financial
plan. You'll be looking at potential inheritances as well as
potential future obligations—necessary information if you are
to get an accurate picture of your financial future. Involving the
generations in financial planning requires total candor among
family members, but it's important for everyone's peace of
mind. If anyone has trouble talking about sticky financial issues
(which often suggests deeper family dynamics), you may benefit
from a meeting or two with a professional counselor.

YOUR SITUATION IS UNIQUE

Periodically you will see statistics such as "two-thirds of investors
plan to work during retirement." Some people find these statistics interesting because they like to see where they stand in rela-
tion to others; others find them irrelevant because they have
nothing to do with them. We want to stress that your financial
situation is totally unique and that you should take statistics,
rules of thumb, and one-size-fits-all financial tenets with a grain
of salt. You've probably heard it said that the average retiree
needs an income of 60 to 80 percent of his or her preretirement
income during retirement. If you find this rule of thumb helpful because you don't want to go to the trouble of filling out a
postretirement budget, then go ahead and use it. But if you
plan to travel a lot, go back to school, or finance an expensive
hobby, you may need even more income during retirement
than you had when you were working. If this is the case, the 60
to 80 percent rule doesn't help you at all. So please understand,
when you read generalizations in this book or anywhere else,

that you need to take a closer look to see if the generalizations apply to you. If not, ignore them.

KNOWLEDGE-BASED PLANNING

The information you need is out there. All you have to do is find it. There is no excuse anymore for skipping some essential aspect of financial planning because you don't know where to go for information. For example, everything you could ever want to know about Social Security is now on the Internet. If browsing through all those web pages is not your style, you can always get a phone number (see Chapter 7) and talk to a live person. Or go to a bookstore. Or to the library. Or you can call your accountant, attorney, stockbroker, or insurance agent. Reading books like this will give you an overview of what you need to know, including some specific details on certain matters, but no one source has everything you need for your particular situation. And that's the key to staying informed without going into information overload. Confine your learning to your specific circumstances and find out what you need to know when you need to know it. It's pointless, for example, to memorize all the minimum mandatory IRA distribution rules when you're not even close to 70½. In addition to taking up precious brain cells, the rules could change before you get there. It's important to have some familiarity with the rules, however, so you can plan ahead and arrange your accounts to best advantage. Just don't dwell on details you're not ready for yet. That said, you are hereby granted permission to skip over the sections in this book that you are not interested in learning about right now. And if you encounter a section that is too basic for you, please understand that we are writing to a broad audience that includes people who are just starting to learn about finance. We recommend that you skim over it to make sure you're not missing anything and skip ahead to the parts that apply to you.

THINGS WILL CHANGE

No matter how meticulously you plan your financial future, the one thing you can be sure of is that your plans probably will change. In order to do financial planning, you need to make certain assumptions. Some of these assumptions are easy and seemingly within your control—at what age you plan to retire, how much you spend on basic necessities each month, whether you plan to work during retirement. Other assumptions are nothing more than a shot in the dark—how long you'll live, what rate of return your investment portfolio will earn over the next thirty years, how many more grandchildren you'll have. The inability to make predictions with absolute certainty should not keep anyone from planning ahead. After all, life is supposed to be a mystery. The key to successful planning is to incorporate flexibility into the plan. By checking your plan regularly and factoring in new information as soon as it becomes available, you can achieve that delicate balance between taking control and allowing life to unfold as it was meant to.

WHERE DO YOU STAND TODAY?

WHAT YOU HAVE

The first step in planning your financial future is knowing where you stand today. There are several components to this self-assessment. One is the usual financial stuff—what you own, how much it's worth, where your assets are invested. To find out where you stand, add up everything you own (your assets) and subtract everything you owe (your debts and liabilities). What's left is your net worth. One of the goals of this book is to help you make that number bigger.

WHAT YOU KNOW

Another component of your self-assessment is what you know, or your level of knowledge about financial matters relevant to your situation. You probably already have a pretty good idea of what you need to know. In fact, if you picked up this book after having looked at the table of contents—well, there's your list of need-to-know items right there. Other questions will come to mind as you go along, so it might help to keep a piece of paper handy so you can jot them down as they arise.

What You've Done

A third component of your self-assessment is what you've done or accomplished. Now, these items can range from something as easy (but important!) as updating your IRA beneficiary to something as complex as putting into place an entire estate plan. The checklist at the end of the chapter will give you an idea of the things you may need to do to plan ahead and get your affairs in order.

Financial situation—what do you have and where is it?

If you have a pretty good idea of where you stand without going through the formal process of creating a financial statement, far be it from us to make you fill in little blanks with numbers. However, there's a reason people use financial statements: so everything will appear in one place. If you've got account statements scattered all over the house, you'd have to do some serious paper shuffling to find out how you're doing. But if you have all the latest numbers written down on one sheet of paper, you can check your net worth at a glance and easily track your progress as you go about making your net worth bigger. Also, having everything in one place will allow you to see if you are properly diversified according to the disciplined investment program you're going to start after reading Part II of this book.

At the very least, you'll want to pull all of your papers together and make a list of your accounts so this information will be available to your next of kin in case of an emergency. Of course you don't expect to get hit by a truck tomorrow—nobody does—but if you did, you'd want your spouse/children/attorney to know where your assets are. And if you ever decide to work with a financial advisor, he or she will need to know what you have in order to develop a comprehensive investment program or financial plan. So do everyone a favor. When you're finished reading this book, gather together all of your important papers, including the following:

- Statements of bank and credit union accounts: checking, savings, term accounts

- Statements of investment accounts, including any mutual funds or annuities held outside your brokerage account(s)

- Copies of any stock certificates or bonds in your custody (with a note telling where the original certificates are located)

- Statements of retirement accounts, including 401(k) plans, IRAs, SEP-IRAs, and any pension or profit-sharing plans

- Tax returns

- Safe deposit box information: location of box, location of key, contents of box

- A copy of the deed to your house

- Insurance policies: life, health, disability, auto, house, long-term care, "Medigap," excess personal liability (umbrella)

- A list of the names and phone numbers of your financial advisors: attorney, accountant, stockbroker, insurance agent, financial planner, investment advisor, business manager

- An outline of your family tree, showing parents, siblings, children, and grandchildren

- A copy of your current will or trust (if any)

- Powers of attorney

- Other important documents: birth certificates, passports, adoption documents, military service records, marriage certificate, divorce decree from prior marriage

When you do get around to creating your financial statements, they can be as simple or as elaborate as you wish. The more detailed they are, the more ways you can analyze your financial situation. However, if big-picture information is all you need for now, just concentrate on the two broad categories: net worth and income.

Net Worth

Your net worth is everything you own minus everything you owe. It's a snapshot at a given point in time and almost certainly will be different from the snapshot you take next month or next year. Depending on where you are in life, your net worth will either be rising or falling. If you are still working and contributing to retirement and investment accounts, your net worth should be rising as you build assets for later in life when you'll be pulling money out to live on. If you are already in the withdrawal stage, you may be seeing a gradual decline in net worth from one year to the next. This is nothing to be alarmed about as long as the drawdown is occurring according to plan and not happening too fast.

Income

Unlike your net worth, which is a snapshot in time, your income statement covers a period of time, usually one year. Your income statement shows how much money flowed into and out of your possession during the period in question. You've heard the phrase "easy come, easy go"? Income statements show this better than anything else. If you're one of those people who spends money without thinking about it too much, your income statement can be very revealing. By pulling out canceled checks and credit card bills and putting expenditures into categories, you'll be able to see exactly how much you spent on clothes or cosmetics or greens fees or whatever your particular weakness happens to be. But this is no time to be hard on yourself or your spouse for spending too much money. Right now you're just collecting information so you can make plans for the future. So gather up your last twelve months' worth of bank statements, bills, and canceled checks and add up how much you earned and how much you spent. For the sake of your sanity (and peace in the family), try to be as dispassionate, unemotional, and nonjudgmental about it as possible.

KNOWLEDGE BASE—
HOW MUCH DO YOU KNOW?

Some people live an entire lifetime without understanding very much about finances. Other people are very financially savvy, learning about investments, retirement plans, estate planning, taxes, and insurance as they go through life, increasing and updating their knowledge all the time. Most people fall somewhere in between. They know enough to keep up but feel guilty/nervous/stupid at times because they don't know everything. Well, let us tell you, nobody knows everything. Have you ever looked at the tax code? Do you know how high all the prospectuses of every mutual fund offered in the United States, if placed in one giant stack, would reach? Do you know how many million pages on the World Wide Web are devoted to financial matters? Face it. You'll never know everything. The key to handling this knowledge thing (or lack thereof) is to know what you need to know and to become comfortable with a certain level of ignorance—as long as you are willing and able to obtain information as you need it.

Now, the reason some people remain blissfully ignorant of financial matters is that they have no reason to study up on the subject. If someone else is handling all that stuff for you, why should you go to the trouble of reading dry, boring financial books and straining your brain to learn about tax rates and price to earnings (P/E) ratios? People who fall into this category do have a point. If you have nothing to do with managing an investment portfolio, you have no reason to be concerned with P/E ratios, nor should you feel guilty about it. But we've all heard horror stories of people (usually women) who let their spouse take care of all the financial matters and who become totally lost when he dies. Suddenly they become the custodians of all these assets they've never heard of before (what's a mutual fund? what's a REIT?), and they become paralyzed with fear. In some extreme cases, they don't even know how to obtain spending money to buy groceries after their husband's death. They aren't sure whom to trust. (Is the stockbroker who just called trying to rip me off, or is he someone my husband trusted and worked with for years?) They don't know whom to call for advice or even what questions to ask. They feel lost and alone. So at the risk of sounding sexist and authoritarian, we will issue the following warnings:

Wives: Start becoming familiar with your family's financial situation. Know what assets you own and where they are. Find out whose name(s) they are in. Figure out what you would do if your husband died first. Know the names and phone numbers of the advisors your husband has been working with: stockbroker, attorney, accountant, insurance agent, business manager, and others. Better yet, get to know the advisors yourself so you'll feel comfortable working with them on your own if it ever comes to that. Above all, overcome your fear and reluctance about financial matters now, while your husband is here to guide and support you.

Husbands: Understand what it must be like for your wife to be in the dark about the family finances. Help her, guide her, push her, if necessary, into learning what she needs to know to survive on her own. Spend a day going over all of your papers. Schedule joint meetings with your advisors. Keep her updated as you go along by sharing monthly statements and talking about investment decisions. Understand that the learning process will take time and patience, and please, give her that. It doesn't do much good to be meticulous in your financial affairs if everything falls apart after you're gone.

Parents and Children: The same goes for you. *Parents:* You never know when a child or other family member will need to step in and take care of your affairs. Why not make it easy for them by showing them where things are and signing the necessary documents so they can take over if you need them to? *Children:* Start becoming familiar with your parents' financial situation and keep an eye on how they're handling things. And if your knowledge of financial matters is lacking, brush up now, especially on matters affecting people your parents' age, such as Social Security, IRA distributions, estate planning, and the like.

PREPAREDNESS—WHAT HAVE YOU DONE AND WHAT DO YOU NEED TO DO?

The following list is not meant to be exhaustive because everyone's situation is unique. The more complex your financial situation is, the more likely you are to rely on professional advisors for information about what to do and when. But even if you have an entourage of advisors, it's a good idea to stay on top of these things so nothing falls between the cracks. And if you are managing your own finances with little outside help, it is crucial for you to be aware of the various checkpoints so you'll be sure to do the right things at the right time. See if any of the following items belong on your to-do list.

- Do you have an easy-to-use recordkeeping system for keeping track of all your financial matters?

- Have you listed your financial goals and what you want to achieve with your money?

- Do you have a reserve fund for emergencies and unplanned expenses?

- Do you have the right kinds of insurance in the right amounts?

- Have you calculated how much income you will need when you retire (or when you enter the next phase of life, if you plan never to retire)?

- Is your investment portfolio, including regular and retirement accounts, positioned as it should be for your risk tolerance, income needs, tax bracket, and long-term goals?

- Have you determined what your Social Security benefits will be and at what age you will begin collecting?

- Do you know what your work options are later in life and how you can prepare for them now?

- Do you have a will?

- Does your IRA beneficiary designation reflect your current wishes?

This self-assessment is by no means exhaustive. To manage your financial affairs properly as you grow older, you must have, know, and do a lot of things. You must *have* enough assets to generate the income you'll need throughout your lifetime. You must *know* enough to properly manage your affairs or to guide the professionals who will be assisting you. And you must *do* certain things at certain times in order to stay in good financial shape. But first, you need to think about your life and how you really want to live.

CHAPTER TWO

How and Where Do You Want to Live?

Recreation is nothing but a change of work—an occupation
for the hands by those who live by their brains, or for
the brains by those who live by their hands.

—Dorothy Thompson

The spending plan that works for you now could change drastically during retirement. If you're not working anymore, what will you be doing with your time? How much will it cost? The 60 to 80 percent rule (that you'll need 60 percent to 80 percent of your preretirement income during retirement) doesn't work for people with big plans and lavish lifestyles. After all, isn't retirement a time to do all the things you never had time to do when you were working, like travel? Go back to school? Set up an elaborate woodworking shop in your garage?

If your retirement lifestyle is pretty well set—you're past retirement, enjoying life the way it is, and have no desire to change it—you can skip this chapter, unless you want to get some ideas about how you may be able to enrich your life by exploring hobbies and interests you may not have thought about before. If you are still looking forward to retirement and just starting to think about what you'll be doing with your time, read on. This chapter offers lots of ideas for retirement lifestyles. The purpose is to get you thinking about how you really want to live during retirement so you can make an accurate budget and figure out how much income you'll need when you're not receiving a paycheck anymore.

A LOOK AT CREATIVE AGING

The notion of active, involved retirees has become so pervasive in our society it's hardly worth talking about here. People who have worked for a long time at one company no longer feel put out to pasture when they retire at 65. Instead, they are hopping into RVs and sailboats and venturing off to see the world. The bridge-playing, golf-playing, shuffleboard-playing Leisure World resident is almost a cliché today. People are living longer, healthier lives, and they're not slowing down for one minute.

Retirement can be a time for frenzied activity—or it can be a time to pause and reflect. Instead of running off to the next scheduled activity, why not take a moment to think about your purpose in life and what remains to be done? What skills and talents lie just under the surface, waiting to be tapped? Who in your circle of family and friends needs your love, support, guidance, or simple presence? How can you turn your wisdom and experience into a gift to the world?

Today's enlightened retirees are asking themselves these questions as they seek to make the last third of their lives even more meaningful than the first two-thirds. In the book *From Age-ing to Sage-ing* (Warner, 1997), Zalman Schachter-Shalomi admits to feeling depressed as he approached his sixtieth birthday. After a forty-day retreat during which he spent most of his time in solitude, he realized he was sloughing off an old phase of life that he had outgrown. At the same time, he saw himself "being initiated as an elder, a sage who offers his experience, balanced judgment, and wisdom for the welfare of society." To initiate the process he asked himself, "If I had to die now, what would I most regret not having done?" The first thing he did was sit down and write loving, heartfelt letters to his children.

He also set new priorities for his professional life and personal relationships. When he returned from the retreat, he had "a new spring in my step and a buoyancy in my heart." He then went on to found the Spiritual Eldering Institute, which sponsors nondenominational workshops to "help people become elders within our modern culture."

After you've taken the time to examine your life and identify spiritual callings, how about exploring some new talents and interests? If bridge, golf, and shuffleboard are all you've ever known, why not pick up a paintbrush and see what happens? If you're retiring from a career that has utilized your analytical skills for thirty years, why not try piano lessons? If you've spent the first two-thirds of your life looking down at the ground, why not buy a telescope and look up at the stars? The number of hobbies and interests available today is astronomical. All you have to do is buy a book, take a class, join an organization, buy the necessary supplies, and throw yourself into it. Speaking of buying the necessary supplies, the purpose of this chapter is to get you thinking about these things so you can build your hobby expenditures into your budget. If you're content with a walk in the woods, no problem. But if you'll be gravitating toward fine wines, classic cars, expensive antiques, or state-of-the-art gadgetry, you'll want to build these indulgences into your budget. No one says you can't have them. You just have to figure out a way to pay for them.

And one way to pay for them is by working. Working??? Yes, lots of people work during retirement—even people who don't need the money. Working is one of the easiest ways to contribute your skills and experience to the world because our capitalistic system is already set up that way. There's nothing more frustrating to a person who wants to give something back to the world after an illustrious career than to be unable to find an outlet for his or her gift. Volunteerism works for some. But just because you're receiving a paycheck doesn't mean your contribution is any less valuable. In some ways, retirees need to change old ways of looking at the world. Quietly holding the hand of a hospice patient is indeed a noble act. So is teaching a young apprentice how to earn an honest living—even if you get paid for doing it.

What will you be doing with your time?

So let's assume that out of a twenty-four-hour day, you'll spend eight hours sleeping, two hours eating (won't it be nice to linger over lunch, perhaps squeezing in a short nap afterward?), one hour showering and other personal care activities, one hour doing some form of exercise, and two hours running errands and doing household chores. What do you have left? About ten hours that you used to spend driving to work, working all day, and driving home from work. Whatever will you do with your time, now that you don't have to do *that* anymore?

We have divided your possible activities into three categories: (1) hobbies and leisure activities, including education and travel; (2) spending time with family and friends; and (3) working, including volunteer work. Now, some people will want to spend almost all of their time in one category. If your career has you totally burned out, you have no family nearby, and are sick of all your friends, you may want to be self-indulgent for a while: Pick a hobby you like, throw yourself into it, and don't apologize to anybody. If, on the other hand, you've been retired for some time and are getting tired of the same old routine, you may want to diversify your life by balancing your time among all three categories. In any case, check out the following sections for some ideas on how to make the most of your time.

Hobbies and Leisure Activities

Hobbies and Interests

When it comes to finding hobbies and leisure activities, it really pays to be open-minded and creative. Rosey Grier, the former football player, was famous for his unabashed enjoyment of needlework. He'd take his needlepoint wherever he went and extol the benefits of the peace and relaxation he derived from a quiet activity that kept his hands busy and resulted in an attractive finished work. Ask other people about their hobbies. You'll learn things you never would have expected about activities you might never have considered—but that could be perfect for you now that you have the time to enjoy them.

Education

The best part about going back to school when you're older is that you're doing it on your terms. You're in it for the knowledge at least as much as the credits, and you're not distracted by the things that once consumed you in school. (You know what they were.) If you've decided to pursue a degree, you've picked a field you know you love, and you look forward to going to class, doing the reading, and even writing papers and taking tests. How different school is today! If you're not pursuing a degree but simply taking classes you're interested in, you can really make the most of the experience. You can do outside reading on your own to enhance what you're learning in class. (Would you ever have done that when you were young?) You can skip class if you don't feel like going. You can even drop a class and not feel guilty.

Travel

There are reasons why so many people like to travel in retirement. The most obvious is that with fewer obligations, they now have the time to take extended vacations. Another reason is that after staying in one place so long, they're eager to see different sights and experience different cultures. The wanderlust hits. Traveling in retirement is very different from those two-week vacations you take while you're working. Unlike the working person, who wants to lie on the beach and have nothing more to do than lift the little umbrella that stands in the way of taking the next sip of piña colada, the retiree is on the move. For retirees, traveling is a time of activity—seeing the sights, learning the history, shopping for rare finds, tasting the food, talking with the locals, and soaking up all that is new and different. For retirees, traveling is both education and hobby—and there's often nothing relaxing about it.

One way to combine education and travel is through Elderhostel, an organization that offers programs on college campuses. A typical program lasts five to six nights, all meals are provided, and there are three or four hours of instruction each day. Over 270,000 people participate at Elderhostel programs at nearly 2,000 educational institutions throughout the United States each year. For more information contact:

Elderhostel
75 Federal Street
Boston, MA 02110
617-426-8056
www.elderhostel.org

Spending Time with Family and Friends

Spending time with family and friends ranks high on many retirees' list of things to do. What once might have seemed a waste of time when you were working and had a more goal-directed mind-set seems a quality activity now that you value relationships more. Sitting on a park bench watching your grandson climb the monkey bars. Sitting by an elderly parent's hospital bed in the middle of the night. Sitting with an old friend who may not have much to say but is enormously grateful that you're there to listen. Our personal relationships are probably our most valuable assets, and one of most beautiful aspects of growing older is that we have the time to enjoy them. Whether you travel cross-country to connect with old school friends or arrange simple get-togethers with people nearby, do make an effort to establish and maintain personal relationships. In the end, they're what matter the most.

Working (for Pay or Not)

More and more, people are viewing their work as a source of fulfillment and are not ready to give it up entirely when they retire. A part-time job or a home-based business that's not too demanding can round out an otherwise carefree existence by putting meaning and purpose in your life. And that is the key to a successful postretirement career. Your work must be meaningful. You must feel as if you are making a valuable contribution to the world in some way.

This has more to do with attitude than with the job itself. Every job has meaning, otherwise it wouldn't exist. Floors must be swept, french fries must be served, shoppers must be helped, and the person who can perform these functions with integrity and joy is indeed making a contribution to the world. If you can find or create work that builds on your lifetime of skills and experience, so much the better—whether it's some lucky nonprofit organization that gets your services for free or a company that appreciates your talents and is willing to pay you what you're worth. Chapter 11 discusses postretirement employment in more detail as a source of income.

WHERE WILL YOU LIVE?

Choosing a retirement location is one of the most important decisions you'll make because it determines both quality of life and cost of living. As you think about where you want to live during retirement, consider taking a fresh look at where you are now. You may take certain characteristics of your neighborhood for granted now but will miss them if you no longer have them. There may also be qualities to your present residence that you currently do not take advantage of because you're too busy working but that would provide tremendous pleasure if you had time to enjoy them. Noontime lectures at the local university or weekday afternoon concerts are examples of activities that might be available in your city that could enrich your retirement lifestyle.

And if you've always assumed you'd stay where you now live after retirement, you may want to rethink that assumption too. Sure, you may be happy there. But perhaps other communities have more to offer. Since your life is going to change anyway, one more disruption won't make that much difference, and you'll be settled in your new community in no time—providing it's the right place for you.

CHOOSING A NEW LOCATION—
BY THE NUMBERS OR BY FEEL?

The latest edition of the *Places Rated Almanac* (Simon & Schuster, 1993) provides a wealth of information about cities and towns across the United States. It's full of statistical data concerning climate, crime rates, cost of living, recreation, and proximity to jobs, educational institutions, health care facilities, and the arts. It even starts out with a quiz to help you assess your priorities. For example, it might ask which is more important to you: local medical specialists who see patients or prospects for white-collar job growth? After taking the quiz and plotting your results on a graph, you can zero in on the areas that interest you and find out which communities rate highest in those areas. If you're a numbers person, you'll love this approach. You can see what the average high temperature is in the summer, how many inches of rain fall in an average year, how many robberies are committed in an average year, and zillions of other statistics.

The advantage of working with numbers is that they're clear-cut and unambiguous. They provide an easy way to rank the various places with no guesswork or "fuzzy thinking" involved. Phoenix is hotter than Duluth in the summer; there's no question about it because the numbers say so.

But numbers can never tell how you will *feel* in a place once you've moved there. You can choose the most ideal location statistically and still be miserable. The reason may be hard to explain. Impossible, even. And that's why statistical analysis should be used as a starting point only, not the definitive answer on the best place to live. Imagine moving to a place that, according to the numbers, is perfect in all respects—it has a temperate climate, low crime, good access to health care, recreation . . . everything else your data sheet said was important to you—yet you're still unhappy. When you try to explain it you can't; all you can point to are the beautiful numbers that deny your feelings and tell why you should be happy. So you stick it out and miss the experience of living in what might have been the perfect community even though it didn't measure up statistically.

It's important that you visit a community several times before moving there. Go at different times of the year, and on your visits imagine what it will be like to live there. What was once the perfect vacation spot with its slower pace and lack of stress-inducing diversions could turn out to be a colossal bore when you're living there every day and looking for something interesting to do.

Visiting a place often also allows you to establish those connections that make moving to a new community easier. When you already know a few people who share your interests, you can build on those relationships to establish a new circle of friends. You can also begin to develop the routines that make life easy and predictable, like frequenting favorite restaurants or shopping at stores you know and like.

Another reason to visit prospective retirement locations before moving there is to see if the things you thought were important to you really are. You may think that proximity to cultural activities and sporting events is more important than access to jobs. But if there's even a remote possibility you'll go stir-crazy without having meaningful work in your life, you need to think about that *before* you move.

You may also be unaware of how the new circumstances will strike you. If you're sick of cold winters you may think Phoenix, with its 167 days of ninety-degree-plus temperatures would be heaven . . . until you actually feel the heat. Then you may find that warm temperatures aren't all they're cracked up to be.

This is not to say you can't get used to your new location and that you won't go through a period of adjustment. When you've lived in one community for a long time, it can be difficult to give up the things that have become so familiar to you. But often the appeal of these things lies in the familiarity itself, not because they're better in any other way. So when you long to go "back home" because you can't find your way around the new grocery store, keep in mind that after a few more visits you'll know exactly which aisle the cereal is on. Everything now familiar was once strange.

Establishing your own criteria

The reason we wanted you to think about *how* you will spend your time in retirement before thinking about *where* you will spend that time is so you can pick the location that will allow you to do what you want to do. You still can take into account the statistical things that are important to you, like crime, climate, and access to health care, but by envisioning what you will be doing with your time every day, you can pick a place conducive to those activities. So here are some criteria for you to think about when contemplating a permanent move to a new location:

- Proximity to friends and family
- Ability to pursue hobbies and interests
- Proximity to airport
- Scenic beauty
- Urban energy
- Small-town charm
- Multiple homes

Proximity to Friends and Family

We put proximity to friends and family first because it's the easiest to take for granted—until you don't have it. If you live near children and grandchildren and have a long-standing network of friends that you see or talk to regularly, we suggest you think twice about moving. It's hard enough adjusting to a new community, but when you're used to being surrounded by friends, the loneliness that can arise from the sudden lack of company can be overwhelming. On the other hand, if you've never been particularly close to other people and get most of your enjoyment out of work, hobbies, or creative endeavors, proximity to friends and family may not be so important. You decide.

Many retirees who have been separated from children for years take this opportunity to move closer to them. When this is the case, you know that proximity to family and friends is the most important (perhaps only) criterion. If so, you can skip to the next chapter.

ABILITY TO PURSUE HOBBIES AND INTERESTS

Some activities can be done anywhere. Others can't. Not to perpetuate the stereotype, but many retirees really do enjoy playing golf. Their wildest dream, now that they're retired, is to play challenging courses several times a week and get their handicap down to 2. If that's your dream too, you'll put "good, challenging golf courses" on your list of criteria when searching for a retirement community and have an awful lot of fun checking them out.

If you are interested in getting better at the things you like to do, you'll also want to check out the availability of classes, workshops, and associations related to your area(s) of interest so you can stay current. Oil painting, for example, can be done anywhere, but if you want to get better at it, you may want to attend classes at a local college.

PROXIMITY TO AIRPORT

No matter how much you like to travel, getting to the airport probably is not high on your list of fun things to do. If you have to drive three hours before your trip can even begin, one of two things will happen: (1) you'll be crabby and disgruntled at the start of every vacation, or (2) you'll take fewer vacations. If you like to go places on airplanes, put "proximity to major airport" high on your list of criteria. That lets out some of the small cities across America, but if you're traveling a lot you're probably seeing plenty of small-town charm in your travels.

SCENIC BEAUTY

Do you crave nature? Does your soul need a daily walk on the beach or view of the mountains to feel grounded and complete? Do you feel at peace in the wide-open spaces? In the desert? In the forest? The power of place is one of those indescribable, undefinable influences on health and well-being that is difficult to measure but has an enormous impact on quality of life. This is especially true as we grow older, start slowing down, and begin to notice the subtle signs of nature and their effect on the way we feel. Trust those feelings. If they conflict with what the statistics say you *should* want in a retirement community, let your feelings override the data and allow your soul to go where it needs to be.

URBAN ENERGY

There are a lot of negative things to say about today's cities—crime, traffic, graffiti, polluted air, crowded living spaces, people of assorted mental capacities living on the streets. There's also an energy that can't be found anywhere else. Major cities are still the nation's art and cultural meccas, housing the best museums, great theater, the finest restaurants, and outstanding shopping. What if you lived just a short walk or cab ride from all this? Would you be willing to put up with the downside of city life—perhaps even see that it's not so awful after all but rather a slice of life that is rich with variety? Many retirees, once they finish raising their children in the suburbs, crave the energy and diversity of the city. It's a chance to change their lifestyle completely and be close to the best the city has to offer. The statistics will tell you it's no place to live, but confirmed city-dwellers would say otherwise.

SMALL-TOWN CHARM

Lots of retirees think a small town is the perfect place to live. It's less stressful than the city, has a real community feel, and is easy to get around in. Plus, there are zillions to choose from. The book *Life in America's Small Cities* by Kevin Heubusch (Prometheus Books, 1997) reports on 193 "micropolitan" areas throughout the United States, including Prescott, Arizona; Vero Beach, Florida; Rutland, Vermont; and Wenatchee, Washington. Like *Places Rated Almanac*, the book uses a scoring system based on statistical data, but you can use it as a start and fill in the crucial happiness determinant—how you feel when you're there—when you visit. If you're several years away from retirement, you can spend your vacations over the next few years searching for the perfect small town to settle down in and going back to visit the ones that rank high on your list.

MULTIPLE HOMES

If you're having a hard time choosing between city versus small town, warm versus cold, east versus west, don't! Consider having more than one home. Once deemed an extravagance enjoyed only by the very rich, lots of people live part of the year in one location and part in another. Some people spend six months in New York and six months in Florida. Others spend nine months in Arizona and head north for the summer, when it gets too hot. Some people spend the week in the city and the weekend in the country—or vice versa. Some people have a large home in one location and a cabin in another. Others have a small house in one location and a lavish condo in the other.

Choosing a place to live is a key part of the retirement planning process because it determines both how you will live your life and what your financial requirements will be. By viewing the process as an exciting adventure, you'll even get some great vacations out of it. Once you've decided where you will live and how you will spend your time, you can start thinking about how much it will cost to live your dream life.

CHAPTER THREE

How Much Will It Cost to Live?

I haven't heard of anyone who wants
to stop living on account of the cost.

—Kin Hubbard

I f you are already retired, do not plan to move, and will not be changing your lifestyle anytime soon, your current spending plan probably will serve you for at least the next several years. If you've been living this way for a while, you obviously have a pretty good handle on your expenses and have managed to balance the income and outgo in a way that works for you. Still, it wouldn't hurt to read over this chapter so you can be thinking ahead and watching for possible changes in your retirement income needs.

This chapter is really designed for people who are still planning and want to know how much income they'll need during retirement. We've all heard of people who fail to plan and are forced to let financial circumstances dictate their lifestyle. They get to retirement, see how much money they have, and then spend as much as the income will allow, sometimes being forced to reduce their standard of living. The preferred way to plan for retirement is to start early, ignore economic reality when deciding how you want to live, and then see how much it will cost to have the lifestyle you envision. If you find you have sufficient resources, great. If not, you may have to start paring back your dreams and aspirations. But if you start planning early enough, you may be able to gather the resources you need for the lifestyle you desire, either by working harder or investing smarter—in other words, by making sacrifices today in order to ensure comfort and security tomorrow.

LOOKING TOWARD THE FUTURE— HOW WILL YOUR EXPENSES CHANGE?

If you took a hard look at your expenses as suggested in Chapter 1, you have a good idea of where your money is going now— or at least where it went over the past twelve months. You may have decided, from that possibly painful exercise, that you want to make some changes to your spending program even before you retire. Are you spending too much on meals out? If so, in your new budget you'll want to redirect some of that money to the savings category. (While we are trying not to be too preachy about the need to save for retirement, figuring you already know that, sometimes we can't help ourselves.) Part of this exercise is also to consider your income over the next twelve months and adjust your expenses accordingly.

So the first step is to go over your current spending plan and make changes where appropriate. The rest of this chapter discusses the various expense categories and how they may change in the future so you can estimate what they will be in retirement. Estimating expenses is not an exact science, but when it comes to knowing your retirement income needs, a guess is better than no clue at all. If it turns out you need to be more aggressive in your saving and investing, you want to know that now, not when you go to cash in those certificates of deposit, whose yields failed to keep up with inflation over the years.

WHAT TO DO ABOUT INFLATION

Speaking of inflation, you're probably wondering how to factor it into your retirement budget so you won't run short later on when you're living on a fixed income. We wish we had an easy answer to this question. You could just pick a number and assume that overall, your expenses will go up by, say, 3 percent a year. But since prices in all categories don't rise at the same rate, the more accurate way to factor inflation into your budget is to consider each category and estimate how much prices will rise in the future due to inflation. Some of the categories will be easy. If you have a fixed mortgage payment, for example, you know it won't be affected by inflation. But just about everything else is subject to inflation, especially items like health care and travel—just the things you'll be spending money on in retirement.

If you want to know what inflation has been in the past for such categories as housing, food, transportation, and medical care, you can ask the U.S. government, which publishes such statistics. (Also see Chapter 14.) In addition to releasing the one inflation number everybody focuses on—the Consumer Price Index (CPI), which lumps all the categories together and tells how much prices changed for an entire basket of goods and services—the government also breaks down the categories and tells how much housing costs rose, how much food costs rose, and so on.

But there's one big problem with looking at past CPI numbers and extrapolating them into the future: Big price changes, either up or down, may be more likely *not* to continue at the same pace. According to the law of supply and demand, there's a limit to how much prices can go up before consumers revolt and refuse to buy. This causes prices to come back down again. But even the law of supply and demand may not be economic gospel anymore. The marketplace is more complex, primarily due to the impact of technology, and it is very difficult to predict even what we'll be buying in the future, much less how much things will cost.

So our recommendation is this: When estimating your expenses in retirement, use today's dollars. They are much easier to work with, and you won't have to try to guess what the future inflation rate for each expense category will be. HOWEVER, in exchange for making your life easier, you have to promise to do two things: (1) You will redo your projected retirement expense budget every year, and if you see prices rising in a particular category adjust the budget accordingly; and (2) when positioning your investment portfolio, you will consider the overall inflation rate and seek investment returns in excess of that rate. It's not a perfect way to deal with inflation, but it's better than nothing. Inflation is impossible to predict, but it's deadly to ignore, as anyone living on a fixed income during the 1970s would tell you.

EXPENSE CATEGORIES—WHAT IS LIKELY TO CHANGE IN THE FUTURE?

Here are some things to think about when creating your post-retirement budget:

- Housing
- Food
- Transportation
- Medical and dental
- Clothing and personal items
- Recreation/travel/education
- Debt payments
- Charity/support of relatives
- Insurance
- Income taxes
- Savings

HOUSING

Mortgage/rent

Utilities

Property taxes

Insurance

Repairs and maintenance

New furnishings and appliances

Your housing costs could stay pretty much the same, or they could change dramatically, depending on how and where you want to live. If you will be staying in the same house, estimating expenses in this category will be easy (but don't forget to factor in major repairs like a new roof or plumbing as your house ages). If you plan to pull up stakes at retirement and transfer the equity in your present home to a new house in a different location, you will need to do the calculations to estimate what your new housing costs will be. This should actually be part of your research when choosing a retirement location. Since housing costs can vary significantly from one area to the next, you may want to name "reasonable housing costs" as one of your search criteria, especially if you're worried about having enough income during retirement. For information on home prices, property taxes, utility costs and other costs of home ownership, contact local real estate agents in the areas you're interested in.

FOOD

Groceries

Meals out

Some things to think about when estimating food costs in retirement: If you work and currently are eating lunch out every day, the $5 to $15 you spend five times a week will stay in your wallet. That amounts to $1,250 to $3,750 per year. A year's worth of tuna-fish sandwiches at home would cost about $325. Throw in an apple and you're up to $400. Your dinner patterns may change too. If you eat out a lot now because you're too tired to cook after working all day, you'll save even more. A home-cooked steak dinner for two—with good wine and all the trimmings—costs about $20. The same meal in a nice restaurant would be at least $60, not counting tax and tip. On the other hand, if eating out is also a form of entertainment, and especially if you'll be traveling a lot, your food costs could stay the same or go up.

TRANSPORTATION

>Car payments (loan or lease)
>
>Car insurance
>
>Gas and oil
>
>Maintenance and repairs
>
>Parking fees
>
>Tolls, public transportation fees

As with lunches out, your transportation costs could change dramatically after you stop working. Instead of commuting X miles a day, your typical daily excursion might be the 1.2 miles to the grocery store or post office. If right now you have two cars in the family, you may be able to get by on one. On the other hand, you might decide to buy a gas-guzzling RV and log twice as many miles in a year as you did when you were working. (RV-related expenses could also go under travel; just be sure you put them somewhere.)

MEDICAL AND DENTAL

>Health and disability insurance premiums
>
>Doctor and dentist bills not covered by insurance
>
>Prescriptions
>
>Glasses, wheelchairs, and other medical items

If your employer currently pays a good chunk of your insurance premiums, your overall medical and dental costs could change significantly after you stop working—not to mention the fact that when people get older, they usually require more medical treatment. Medicare will kick in at age 65, but if you plan to leave your job before then, you'll have to pay for health insurance yourself until you qualify for Medicare. If this is the case, find out what the rates will be so you can plan ahead. Although there's no way of knowing what kind of medical treatment you'll need as you grow older, you may want to pick a number—say 25 percent—and increase your expected medical expenditures by that amount. If you don't need it, you can celebrate your good health by allocating unspent medical money to the recreation and travel category.

CLOTHING AND PERSONAL ITEMS

> Clothes and shoes
>
> Cosmetics and hair salon services
>
> Dry cleaning, tailoring

What we just said about working and lunches? Ditto for clothes. No more suits. No more expensive shoes. No more dry cleaning. On the day you retire, go to the nearest department store and stock up on soft, comfortable clothes. That should take care of your postretirement clothing budget for a couple of years anyway. Clothes are not usually a big deal for retirees. You're not out to impress people anymore, and the more times you wash your favorite outfits, the more comfortable they become. You might even make some money by selling your working wardrobe to a consignment shop or donating it to charity for a tax write-off.

RECREATION/TRAVEL/EDUCATION

> Hobbies
>
> Travel
>
> Entertainment
>
> Classes, educational expenses
>
> Gifts/holiday expenses

This is the big mystery category that could change dramatically after you retire. All those hobbies and interests you don't have time for now are just waiting to be explored and enjoyed. And only you know to what degree you will be spending money on them. Again, try to envision your life. How many times a week will you be playing golf? Multiply that many days' greens fees by fifty-two, and there's your golf budget (don't forget cart, golf balls, nineteenth hole, etc.). If you don't know yet what you want to do or what the costs will be, just put down some generous figure so you'll have plenty of freedom to explore. And keep in mind that travel and recreation items usually cost more than you think they will. Decide how much you think you'll spend, double it, and enjoy.

DEBT PAYMENTS

Personal loans

Credit cards

Won't it be nice to have all your debts paid off at retirement? That at least should be the goal. With the exception of your mortgage, most of your current debts are probably short term anyway, scheduled for full repayment before you retire. With proper planning, your postretirement budget will have a zero in this category.

CHARITY/SUPPORT OF RELATIVES

Charitable contributions

Support of relatives

Here's another category that could be difficult to predict unless you know your family and what its future needs may be. Expenses in this category could include nursing home care for aging parents who lack sufficient resources, helping adult children buy their first home, or contributing to grandchildren's college expenses. Only you know how generous you want (or can afford) to be.

INSURANCE (NOT COVERED IN OTHER CATEGORIES)

> Life insurance
>
> Disability insurance
>
> Long-term care insurance

Since we have devoted a whole chapter to insurance, we won't say much about it here, except that it's a pretty important category for people as they get older. It's not so much that you have dependents to protect (the major reason for buying life insurance when your family is young), but rather to take advantage of the tax benefits for estate planning purposes when your net worth is high. And long-term care insurance is something everyone needs to think about, whether for themselves or a loved one. Keep it in the back of your mind and leave the category blank for now.

INCOME TAXES

Your income tax obligations will change with the amount and type of income you receive. As we have devoted a whole chapter to taxes, leave this category blank for now.

SAVINGS (INCLUDING RETIREMENT PLAN CONTRIBUTIONS)

The simple way to view the retirement bucket is to show contributions going in while you're working and coming out when you're not working. That's generally how it works, but it's often not so clear-cut. Many people continue to save during retirement because their pensions and investments are generating more income than they need. On the other hand, there's no point in receiving taxable income that you don't need if you're just going to turn around and invest it. Better to keep that money working in a tax-deferred retirement account or annuity until you need it. (More on these in Part II.)

Is your spending plan reasonable?

Far be it from us to say if your spending plan is reasonable or not. If you eat dinner out every night and can afford it, it's nobody's business how self-indulgent you want to be—certainly the restaurant owners appreciate it. But it can be interesting to see how your spending plan compares to others'. According to a U.S. Trust Survey of Affluent Americans—the top 1 percent of wealthiest Americans with either an adjusted gross income of more than $200,000 or a net worth greater than $3 million—this is how their expenses broke down (note that the survey did not differentiate between retired and nonretired):

Savings and investments	27%
Housing, utilities, and maintenance	23%
Food and clothing	16%
Vacation and travel	12%
Children's expenses	8%
Charitable contributions	8%
Healthcare and insurance	6%

But again, we want to caution you against using statistics to dictate what's right for you. Outside of the research labs, there's no such thing as an "average American."

Investing

CHAPTER FOUR

Developing Your Primary Source of Retirement Income

Money is a guarantee that we may have what
we want in the future. Though we need nothing
at the moment, it ensures the possibility of
satisfying a new desire when it arises.

—Aristotle

Throughout this book, we are referring to the last third of life as "retirement," even knowing full well that you may continue to work for many years after you leave your primary career. In some respects, the word "retirement" is a misnomer because most people don't "retire" at all. However, what is unique about this time of life is that your sources of income will change. Before retirement, you get a couple of checks a month from one employer. These checks are usually in predictable amounts and come at predictable times. After retirement, you may get lots of different checks from many different sources, including Social Security, corporate pension, and perhaps a part-time job. But your biggest checks may be the ones you write to yourself out of your investment accounts. After all those years of putting money in, it will finally be time to take money out and spend it. This can be a scary proposition if you've disciplined yourself not to touch your investment and retirement accounts because you know they have to last a lifetime. But there comes a time when you're *supposed* to start withdrawing funds from your investment accounts—that's what they're there for—so you may need to shift your mind-set and give yourself permission to pay yourself back for all those years of sacrifice and intelligent investing.

The key to worry-free withdrawals, however, is planning. If you just sit down one day and start writing checks to yourself without having some idea of how much you can take out safely and how long the money will last, one of two things could happen. If you're so worried about outliving your savings, you might make the checks really small and possibly deprive yourself of the comfortable lifestyle you deserve. On the other hand, if you simply spend whatever amount you need without considering how long the money will last, you could be in danger of running out. So you'll need to do some serious planning in order to give yourself the right amount of income while making sure that the bucket doesn't run dry. Chapter 6 goes into this in more detail.

By the way, you may be accustomed to thinking of your retirement and personal investment accounts as your "nest egg." We're not sure why that term has become so popular because when you break an egg it runs all over the place and makes a big mess. When you're ready to start living off your savings and investments, you'll want to have more control over your income stream. You certainly won't want to have it come out all at once, and you may even want to keep adding to it. (It's pretty hard to make a broken egg bigger.) We prefer to use the analogy of a bucket. During your working years you add to the bucket in the form of retirement plan contributions and monthly savings. As the investments build up, they start generating significant contributions of their own, building earnings on top of earnings, sort of like the way yeast makes dough rise without your having to do anything to it. Whenever you receive a lump sum, whether it's an inheritance or a retirement distribution, you add it to the bucket. Your goal is to make the bucket as full as possible. Then when you're ready to start drawing income, you punch a small hole in the bottom of the bucket and siphon off as much as you need. If you plan it right, the money in the bucket will keep rising even as you siphon income off the bottom, so the bucket will never be in danger of becoming empty.

FILLING YOUR RETIREMENT BUCKET: HOW MUCH CAN YOU SAVE BETWEEN NOW AND THEN?

If your bucket is not as full as you think it should be to provide the income you're going to need during retirement, now's the time to accelerate the savings, if possible. If you're in your 50s or 60s and still working, you're probably in your peak earning years. The kids are out of the house, college and wedding expenses are behind you, and the days of scrimping and saving are over. Finally you can make up for all those years when family obligations prevented you from saving as much as you would have liked. And if you decide to get serious about it, you really can make up for lost time. A thousand dollars a month, invested at 10 percent, will grow to $400,000 in fifteen years. When you retire, you could start taking out 8 percent, or $32,000 a year, and leave the rest to grow. That, combined with Social Security, may be all the income you'll need. So the first thing you can do to build your personal savings and investments is to sock away as much money as you can as fast as you can.

The next thing you'll need to do is pay close attention to how your savings are invested. One or two percentage points in investment returns may not seem like much, but compounded over a period of time, it can make a big difference in how much money you'll have at retirement. For example, if you are fifty-five years old now and plan to save $500 a month until you retire at age seventy, you'll have $173,019 at retirement if your investments earn 8 percent. But if they earn 10 percent, you'll have $207,235. See Table 4.1 to find out how much you can accumulate between now and retirement.

TABLE **4.1** **HOW MUCH CAN YOU ACCUMULATE TOWARD YOUR RETIREMENT?**

If You Plan to Retire in Twenty Years

If you are 50 now, this is how much you can accumulate at age 70 if you save:

	6%	8%	10%
$ 100/mo.	$ 46,204	$ 58,902	$ 75,937
$ 500/mo.	231,020	294,510	379,684
$1,000/mo.	462,040	589,020	759,368

If You Plan to Retire in Fifteen Years

If you are 55 now, this is how much you can accumulate at age 70 if you save:

	6%	8%	10%
$ 100/mo.	$ 29,081	$ 34,604	$ 41,447
$ 500/mo.	145,409	173,019	207,235
$1,000/mo.	290,818	356,038	414,470

If You Plan to Retire in Ten Years

If you are 60 now, this is how much you can accumulate at age 70 if you save:

	6%	8%	10%
$ 100/mo.	$ 16,388	$ 18,295	$ 20,485
$ 500/mo.	81,940	91,473	102,422
$1,000/mo.	163,879	182,946	204,845

If You Plan to Retire in Five Years

*If you are 65 now, this is how much you
can accumulate at age 70 if you save:*

	6%	8%	10%
$ 100/mo.	$ 6,977	$ 7,348	$ 7,744
$ 500/mo.	34,885	36,738	38,719
$1,000/mo.	69,770	73,477	77,437

RETIREMENT SAVINGS VEHICLES

In addition to socking money away and earning high returns on
your investments, you'll also want to save taxes wherever you
can. Fortunately, Uncle Sam is very supportive of people who
save for retirement. By utilizing one or more of the savings vehicles that have been set up for this purpose, you can save a bun-
dle in taxes and fill your retirement bucket all the faster.

With some exceptions, most retirement plans offer two key
tax advantages. First, the salary you contribute to the plan is not
subject to current taxes. So if you make $60,000 this year and
contribute $5,000 to a retirement plan, you will report $55,000
in income. That will save you $1,400 in taxes, if you are in the 28
percent federal tax bracket. The second big benefit is that your
investment earnings are not taxable as long as they remain in
the account. This is in contrast to a regular (nonretirement)
investment account, where you have to pay taxes on your investment income every year even if you reinvest the earnings. So
while you're saving for retirement, it makes sense to take advantage of these special types of retirement plans to the fullest
extent possible before putting money into regular taxable savings or investment accounts.

The only restriction on retirement accounts is that if you
take the money out before age 59½, you may have to pay penalties. However, there are ways around that rule (see Chapter 9) if
you retire early or really need the money, so please don't let

early withdrawal rules deter you from taking advantage of these
very special accounts.

EMPLOYER-SPONSORED RETIREMENT PLANS

Employer-sponsored retirement plans are accounts you contribute to while you're working. Your employer may also offer a
traditional pension plan, called a defined benefit plan, that the
company contributes to on your behalf. However, since you
have no control over that account, we will limit our discussion
here to accounts that you may have an opportunity to contribute to, either through your employer or through your own
plan if you are self-employed or own a business.

401(k) and 403(b) Plans

If you work for an employer who offers a 401(k) or 403(b) plan,
you can contribute part of your salary to your own retirement
account according to a schedule set up by your employer. If
you're lucky, your employer will kick in matching funds to
encourage you to contribute. That's free money, which you can
get only by contributing to the plan. We strongly urge you to
push the limit and contribute the maximum you're allowed,
especially if your employer is making matching contributions.

Retirement Plans for Business Owners and Self-Employed Individuals

If you are self-employed or own a business, you can set up your
own qualified retirement plan and make tax-deductible contributions to it. These contributions may be as high as 25 percent
of your salary (to a maximum of $30,000), depending on the
type of plan you set up. Each plan is slightly different in some
way, so think about what is most important to you—high tax
deduction, flexibility in contributions, whether you have
employees—and talk to your tax advisor or retirement plan con-
sultant about which type of plan is best for you. By the way, these
plans are great for people with side businesses—including
retirees who have officially "retired" and want to keep adding to
their retirement bucket.

INDIVIDUAL RETIREMENT ACCOUNTS (IRAS)

The amount you can contribute to an IRA may not be much compared to the many thousands of dollars a year you can sock away in one of the other types of retirement plans, but it does add up. And if you are eligible to tax-deduct your contribution (which you can do if you are not covered by a retirement plan at work), it definitely makes sense to contribute. Each $2,000 contribution, for someone in the 28 percent tax bracket, saves $560 in taxes. And, of course, the investment earnings grow tax-deferred until you take the money out. You must have earned income (investment income doesn't count) and be under age 70½ in order to contribute to a regular IRA.

The new Roth IRA may be a better alternative for some people because the money comes out tax free. You don't get a tax deduction up front for your contribution, but the money grows tax free and you never have to pay taxes on it when you take it out (as long as it's been in there at least five years or you're over 59½). One advantage for retirees is that you can keep contributing past the age of 70½, and there are no minimum mandatory withdrawal rules at that age, as there are with regular IRAs. (See Chapter 9). You do have to have earned income in order to contribute, however. Also, your adjusted gross income (AGI) must be under $110,000 if you are single, or $160,000 if you file a joint return, in order to be eligible.

If you leave your job—whether you're officially retiring or just changing employers—you may be handed your share of the company's retirement plan. Don't take it! Instead, set up an IRA rollover account and tell the employer to send the check there, so you won't have to pay taxes on the distribution and you can keep the money growing tax deferred. See Chapter 8 for more information on converting pension assets to an IRA rollover account.

TAX-DEFERRED ANNUITIES

Once you have (1) maxed out your 401(k) plan, (2) contributed to any qualified retirement plans you may be eligible for as a business owner or self-employed individual, and (3) made your annual $2,000 IRA contribution, you may still want to add to your retirement bucket by saving money in a regular taxable investment account. Before you do that, consider investing in a tax-deferred annuity. Tax-deferred annuities are investments sponsored by insurance companies, and they have been granted special tax status to make them suitable for retirement savings. Similar to an IRA, the investment earnings are not taxable until you take the money out, and you can choose from a variety of investment options.

MAKING YOUR MONEY GROW

Speaking of investment options, let's talk about how you can fill your retirement bucket even faster by letting the money that's in there do some of the work. Think of your retirement bucket as having two components: the money you put in and the money you get through investment returns. When you first start filling the bucket, most of the contents will consist primarily of your own contributions. Later your investment earnings will build up and soon take on a life of their own, generating earnings on top of earnings and growing of their own momentum. Table 4.2 shows how investment earnings outstrip contributions in the later years of saving.

TABLE **4.2** INVESTMENT RETURNS

Contribute $500 per month. Earn investment returns of 10%.

	TOTAL VALUE OF ACCOUNT	AMOUNT FROM CONTRIBUTIONS	AMOUNT FROM INVESTMENT EARNINGS
5 YEARS	$ 38,719	$30,000	$ 8,719
10 YEARS	$102,422	$60,000	$ 42,422
15 YEARS	$207,235	$90,000	$117,235

By the way, when we talk about investing your retirement bucket, we are referring to all of your retirement and investment accounts, including:

- 401(k) plan assets
- Retirement plans you set up as a business owner or self-employed individual
- Contributory IRAs
- Rollover IRAs
- Tax-deferred annuities
- Personal investments acquired through saving, inheritance, sale of home or business, or other windfall

Even though you may have several accounts that have to be kept separate, it's important to consider all of your assets when designing an investment strategy. That's because of this new-fangled approach called Modern Portfolio Theory, which has proven that you can reduce risk and improve returns by coordinating your investments so they all work together as a whole. It's sort of like taking medications. Since one pill can have an effect on another, your doctor/pharmacist/you need to consider how all the pills work together on the system known as your body. So when we refer to your "portfolio," we are talking about making all of the investments work together on the system known as your retirement bucket. While some of your investment returns will be taxable and some won't be depending on the type of account they're in, that doesn't change the basic strategy. Techniques for saving taxes get layered on top of the basic investment strategy and are applied later to the appropriate accounts. You have to get the basics down first.

CHAPTER FIVE

Understanding Investing

Money is a terrible master but
an excellent servant.

—P.T. Barnum

At this point, we're going to take a step back and cover a few basics for the new people. If you've been investing for many years, you can skip this section. But if you have a spouse or parent who is just starting to learn about investments, you may want to walk them through this information, pointing out how the various investment principles apply to your (their) own situation. Financial material is always more meaningful when it transcends the academic and relates to real life.

WHERE INVESTMENT RETURNS COME FROM

Investment returns are the yeast that makes your dough grow. Sorry for the trite and overused analogy, but if you understand that investment returns are money that you earn without your having to do anything (except provide the opportunity for those investment returns to occur), you understand the concept of investing, as opposed to putting your savings into a piggy bank or under a mattress. Investment returns are what you get when you put your money to work.

INTEREST INCOME

Interest income is the easiest to understand. It's what the bank pays you on your savings account. It's what your kids pay you (or not) when you loan them money. It's the income you get if you own a bond or other interest-bearing investment vehicle. Interest income is usually stated as a percentage of the amount invested and is usually an annual rate, even though the interest may be paid quarterly or semiannually. So if you buy a $10,000 bond that pays 7% interest and the interest payments are made semiannually, each year you own the bond you'll get two checks of $350 each, for a total of $700 per year.

One important thing to know if you are considering an interest-bearing investment is whether the interest rate can change. If you invest $10,000 in a ten-year bond with a fixed interest rate of 7%, you know you can count on receiving $700 every year for ten years. On the other hand, if you put your savings into a money market fund or "floating rate" fund, you'll know that the interest rate can change—sometimes as often as daily. Most people use short-term accounts for funds they need to keep liquid and invest in longer-term vehicles when they want to receive regular income over a period of time.

DIVIDENDS

Dividends are checks you receive when you own shares of stock. Maybe. Companies declare dividends when they know what their earnings will be, and since corporate earnings vary, dividends can vary. But dividends can be an important source of income for retirees because of one distinguishing feature: The checks can get bigger over the years. Unlike interest income, which is fixed, dividends can—and often do—increase.

Certain stocks are recognized as dividend-paying stocks, so if dividends are important to you, you'll want to gravitate toward those stocks and start asking questions. First, you'll want to know the *dividend yield.* That's the dollar amount of the dividend per share divided by the price per share. So if a company pays a dividend of $1 per share and the stock is selling at $20 per share, the dividend yield is 5 percent (1 ÷ 20 = .05). If you invest $10,000 in this company, you can expect to receive $500 in dividends the first year. Next, you'll want to know the company's record of increasing dividends. This can be reliable information for estimating whether the company will increase dividends in the future. Finally, you'll want to know if the company has enough earnings to cover the dividends. If the company pays $1 per share in dividends and has only $1.20 per share in earnings, that leaves only 20 cents per share left over for the company to reinvest in the hope of generating more earnings. A company that does not have its dividend very well covered might be in danger of having to decrease it in future years if earnings fail to keep up.

CAPITAL GAINS

Capital gains are what you get when you buy low and sell high. This is the most uncertain type of investment income of all because you can never predict the future price of any asset that trades on the open market, whether it's stocks, bonds, houses or Beanie Babies. Interest income you can be fairly certain of. Dividend income you can be a little more sure of. But capital gains are a shot in the dark, often consisting of nothing more than a hope and a prayer until they are finally realized—that is, when you sell the security and get cash back for it. What makes investing so difficult for some people is when the bulk of their investment returns are expected to come from capital gains and yet there's no way of telling what those capital gains will be. But avoiding investments that pay capital gains can deprive you of a significant source of retirement income. If you try to fill your retirement bucket with interest or dividend income alone, it will take an awfully long time to fill it up; you will barely keep up with inflation. But if you invest in something that offers the opportunity—although no assurance—of capital gains, there's a chance you'll be able to fill your retirement bucket much faster. The key is understanding how the capital gains are derived as well as what conditions might create capital losses, so you can decide for yourself if you want to proceed with the investment.

TOTAL RETURN

You may sometimes hear the term "total return." This term is applied to investments that offer some combination of interest, dividends, and/or capital gains. For example, if you own a stock that pays a 3 percent dividend, and the stock appreciates by 7 percent in one year, your total return for the year is 10 percent. Mutual funds often state their investment earnings as total returns. When evaluating prospective investments, you'll want to know what the total return is composed of. If most of it is interest or dividend income, you'll know that it's pretty reliable income (although the rate of return may be low). If most of it is capital gains, you'll know that you cannot necessarily count on the same returns in the future, because capital gains can be unpredictable.

HOW TO EVALUATE INVESTMENTS

When evaluating investments, you'll want to know something about how the investment returns are generated. Most investments involve some element of risk, or uncertainty, and the best way to evaluate that risk is to know about the underlying fundamentals that create the investment returns. When you understand the inner workings of an investment, you can decide if the risk is worth taking or not.

An example of how knowledge can make people feel comfortable with investing (or not) is revealed in the way corporate employees choose investments for their 401(k) plans. Most employees tend to stick with what they know, picking either "stable value funds," which are similar to the bank savings accounts they've grown up with, or their own company's stock. Now, there's no reason in the world why their own company's stock should be a better investment than any other company's stock, but employees choose it because they are familiar with the company. They know the people, the products, the customers—in other words, they know how the company makes its money. And even though the stock price may fluctuate, they feel comfortable investing in it because they know the company will be around tomorrow.

Now, granted, when you work for a company you know a lot more about it than any investment you may be considering from afar. We are not suggesting that you restrict your investing to securities with which you have that kind of intimate knowledge. In fact, often we have to encourage 401(k) investors to look beyond their own backyard and choose a more diversified selection of investments in order to reduce their overall level of risk. But when presented with an investment opportunity, do try to learn more about it by asking the following three questions.

1. What is the expected rate of return?

2. What factors influence these investment returns?

3. What can go wrong?

Now, we do not want to make investing any more complicated than it needs to be, but once you get into this you'll find that the answers to these questions cannot always be stated in twenty-five words or less. You'll hear a lot of "if this happens, then that will happen, but if that happens, then this will happen." We must caution you against trying to distill everything down to one simple answer. That's how people get blindsided ("but the nice man told me I'd make 25 percent on my money; he never said I could lose it").

1. WHAT IS THE EXPECTED RATE OF RETURN?

Of the three questions, this is the one you'll have the hardest time getting a straight answer to. And that's a good thing. If someone does give you a straight answer, and if it's very much higher than the current rate on U.S. Treasury bills, run the other way because there's something he's not telling you. The

Treasury bill rate is the benchmark for risk-free returns. When the U.S. government promises to pay you a certain rate of interest and to give you your money back in three months or six months (or whatever term Treasury bill you're buying), you can darn sure believe it. Anybody else is suspect, unless he or she also has the ability to print money.

This is not to say U.S. Treasury bills are necessarily good investments. Because they are risk-free, they pay fairly low returns, somewhere around the inflation rate or slightly above. When you're investing for retirement, you want your investment returns to exceed the rate of inflation by a pretty good margin to cover rising income needs during retirement. Thus you must move beyond the realm of risk-free investing and consider investments offering the potential for higher returns.

But often these returns cannot be forecasted in advance, especially if capital gains figure into the equation. And to make matters worse, there's a regulatory paradox that misleads the very investors the regulators are trying to protect. The paradox has to do with how investment companies are allowed to state investment returns. Because they are prohibited from projecting future returns, investment sponsors can only talk about the past. So when you ask, "What is the expected rate of return?" you'll be told something like "Over the past fifteen years, this mutual fund has provided an average annual return of 15 percent." Investment representatives who tell you this are not ducking your question—they are only telling you what they are allowed to say. But historical returns tell you nothing about the future. And they can be very misleading. Although the words "past performance is no guarantee of future results" must appear somewhere in the pitch, often it's in very fine print and easily overlooked. So after you're told the historical rate of return, listen for what comes next. Does the representative leave it at that and let you assume that the returns of the past will continue into the future? Or does he or she go on to explain how investment returns are derived and discuss the outlook for those factors having the biggest influence on investment returns?

2. WHAT FACTORS INFLUENCE THESE INVESTMENT RETURNS?

Given that in many cases we can't know exactly what the expected returns of an investment will be, how do we go about evaluating it? And why? Why not stick with what we know, as so many 401(k) participants do when they choose stable-value funds or their own company's stock? Second question first. The reason you do not want to stick just with what you know is that you don't know enough yet. No offense, but it's simply too risky to put all your eggs in the one or two baskets you have an intimate knowledge of. You may think you're taking the least risky route, but that's only because of your limited perspective. There's a whole universe of investments out there, and by spreading your money among them, you increase your chances of earning more and losing less. More on diversification and asset allocation in Chapter 6.

To see what factors may have an influence on investment returns, let's look at the three types of investment income—interest, dividends, and capital gains. Interest income is the easiest to understand since it is usually clearly stated in the investment description. For example, if you buy $10,000 worth of XYZ bonds paying 8 percent interest and maturing on October 1, 2009, you can pretty much count on receiving interest payments of $800 per year and your $10,000 back on October 1, 2009. This is assuming XYZ keeps its promise, of course. You can get an idea of XYZ's creditworthiness by checking the bond's rating. AAA is the highest, AA is next highest, and it goes down from there. If you stick with investment-grade bonds rated BBB or higher, your interest checks should come as promised.

Dividend income directly relates to corporate earnings. It is also clearly stated, although it can change from one quarter to the next. Dividend-paying companies typically raise their dividends when earnings are up and lower their dividends when earnings are down. Although it may be difficult for you to predict a company's future earnings, securities analysts do it all the time. You can obtain their research reports through brokerage firms and stock research services. By the way, you will not find earnings predictions in a company's annual report; companies are prohibited by law from forecasting their earnings. Generally speaking, a strong economy and positive outlook for the industry are favorable for earnings, while a sluggish economy and negative outlook are unfavorable. There may also be factors unique to a particular company that can positively or negatively affect earnings.

Not to confuse the issue here, but mutual funds often state their distributions as dividends, even though the investment returns are derived from capital gains, not stock dividends. Therefore, mutual fund dividends may not be as predictable as you think; to check, you'll have to dig into how the capital gains are derived.

The factors influencing capital gains are what you will be most interested in watching, because, as we've noted, capital gains are impossible to predict with certainty. However, by understanding some of the forces at work, you can have some idea of what *could* happen. Then you'll be able to look at individual investments with more objectivity and also understand the reasoning behind the investment strategy outlined in Chapter 6, which considers how groups of investments work together to balance each other and reduce overall risk.

In general, you get capital gains (or losses) from buying and selling assets that trade on the open market. At its most fundamental level, each market operates according to the law of supply and demand. When an item is in high demand, its price goes up. When it is in low demand, its price goes down. What matters to you as an investor is not necessarily what the demand for your investment will be tomorrow or the next day but what it will be when you are ready to sell it.

Bond Prices

Bond prices are affected by interest rates. If you buy a bond that pays 8 percent, and a year after you buy it the interest rate on similar bonds is 9 percent, your bond will not be in very high demand. So in order to sell your bond, you'd have to discount the price to make the interest payments yield 9 percent to a new investor. However, if you plan to hold the bond until maturity, you won't have to discount it because you will not be entering the marketplace where the law of supply and demand is at work. You'd simply hold onto your bond, collect the interest payments, and ignore any fluctuations in market price. Remember, you are interested in assessing the potential for capital gains (or losses) *at the time you are ready to sell the security.* Most people buy bonds with the intention of holding them to maturity and therefore need not be concerned with daily price fluctuations.

Stock Prices

At the risk of oversimplifying stock market dynamics, we'll say that the price you can expect to get for a stock depends in part on when you want to sell it. On a long-term basis, stock prices usually reflect corporate earnings. So if you buy stock in a company that makes a good product, is in a growing industry, is well managed, and has all the other elements that generally produce higher earnings year after year, there's a pretty good likelihood that when you go to sell your shares, you'll get more than you paid for them. On the other hand, if you buy a stock today and go to sell it tomorrow, there's no telling what you'll get. The forces that influence the market on a day-to-day basis can be anything from wild rumors to unfounded fears. That's why it's important for you, as a long-term investor, to keep your eyes focused on the more distant future and not let daily price fluctuations drive you crazy. Chances are, when you are ready to sell your stocks, you will receive a higher price than you paid because the companies you invested in will have done very well and made lots of money during the time that you owned them.

Mutual Fund Shares

Mutual funds are simply a vehicle for investing in stocks and/or bonds. So to understand the factors that influence changes in the price of mutual fund shares, you need to look at what the fund invests in. If it invests in small-company stocks, for example, the price of each mutual fund share will be quite volatile, because small-company stocks are usually quite volatile. If it invests in a portfolio of intermediate-term bonds, its price will likely be more stable. Again, we want to caution you against assuming that the returns of the past will continue into the future. The only way mutual funds can legally state investment returns is to use historical data. Take it with a grain of salt and start asking questions about the fund's investment strategy.

3. WHAT CAN GO WRONG?

Your assessment of the factors influencing investment returns should include both positive and negative items, but in case the bad stuff never comes up, be sure to ask specifically what can go wrong. Although you won't want to dwell on the negative, you will want to know what the chances are of losing money so you can decide for yourself if the risk is worth taking.

CHAPTER SIX

Managing Your Investments

With money in your pocket, you are wise and you
are handsome and you sing well, too.

—Jewish Proverb

INVESTING YOUR LIFE SAVINGS: LESSONS LEARNED FROM THE PAST

Twenty years ago it was common for retirees to invest all of their savings in short-term vehicles. People would take their lump-sum distribution to their local bank or brokerage firm and ask where they could get the highest "yield." At that time, it was thought that the higher the "yield," the more income the retiree would receive. So people shopped around for the "best deal," looking for the account that "paid the most." In the late 1970s and early 1980s, money market funds and certificates of deposit were "paying" around 12 percent (briefly, they even reached 18 percent). What did this mean for the retiree? It meant that a lump-sum distribution of, say, $300,000 would generate interest income of $36,000 a year, or $3,000 a month. Retirees who could live on this amount could leave the $300,000 intact and live off the interest. That was the goal of every retiree: to be able to live off the interest and leave the principal intact.

Then something unexpected happened. Interest rates went down. The 12 percent "yield" that paid the rent and bought the groceries dropped to 10 percent, then 8 percent, then 6 percent, then 4 percent. Retirees who were counting on $3,000 a month had their income slashed to $1,000 a month. And to make matters worse, prices were creeping up at the same time due to inflation. So retirees were hit with a double whammy: lower income and higher expenses. The only solution was to dip into principal, which was the last thing retirees wanted to do.

Meanwhile, people who hadn't retired yet, who were still building their investment portfolio for the future, didn't worry so much about "yield" or keeping their "principal intact." Since they were reinvesting their investment returns anyway, they didn't treat their principal as a sacred object not to be touched. All that mattered was that their account balance kept getting bigger over time. This relaxed attitude about principal enabled them to—egad!—put it at risk. They did this by buying stocks. Some stocks went up while others went down. But over the last twenty years more have gone up than down, so that people who invested in stocks in the late 1970s earned overall returns of more than 17 percent, compared to those yield-oriented retirees who, if they were lucky enough to be able to leave their principal untouched, earned an average of less than 7 percent.

This unfortunate turn of events was not the fault of the retirees. Most people retiring at that time had lived through the Great Depression. They saw how devastating stock market losses could be. And since stocks had pretty much drifted sideways during the 1960s and 1970s, they didn't see how stocks could benefit them very much. The risk/return ratio did not appear favorable, especially when they could get 12 percent without putting their principal at risk. If they could have known in advance how the scenario would play out, they would have done things quite differently.

So where does that put you, the soon-to-be-retiree who is willing to learn from the mistakes of the past but certainly can't afford to make any new mistakes of your own? Well, first you'll want to review the lessons we've learned over the past fifty years or so and then put everything into perspective as you look ahead to your own future. Here are some of the things we've learned about investing:

- The stock market crash of 1929 is unlikely to happen again because of safeguards that have been built into the system, such as more stringent margin requirements.

- Yields on short-term vehicles, such as certificates of deposit and money market funds, fluctuate over time. They are not suitable for long-term investors seeking a predictable income stream.

- Investments involve varying degrees of risk. The key is knowing your own risk tolerance and finding investments you feel comfortable with.

- There's nothing sacred about principal. The idea is to keep the bucket full enough to generate the income you need. Who cares if the contents of the bucket are made up of principal, interest, dividends, or capital gains? It's all money.

- Nobody can predict the stock market or the direction of interest rates. The only way to cope with this forced ignorance is to diversify your portfolio among several types of assets so if one investment goes down, the others, it is hoped, are going up.

- Investing can be an emotionally charged experience. It's natural to feel the emotions; just don't let them cloud your judgment.

FOUR STEPS FOR MANAGING YOUR INVESTMENT PORTFOLIO

There are four steps to managing an investment portfolio. If you're just getting started or have been accustomed to picking investments by the seat of your pants, you may be interested in knowing how the professionals do it. Why follow a disciplined plan? Because when you don't, you end up with a bunch of investments you don't even like anymore and aren't sure why you bought in the first place. And without a plan, it's easy to become discombobulated when the market drops, because you have nothing telling you whether you should sell, hold, or buy more. A disciplined strategy sets you on course in the beginning and provides direction when the unexpected happens or when emotions threaten to ruin best-laid plans.

STEP 1: DETERMINE YOUR INVESTOR PROFILE

As you go about the task of gaining investment knowledge, your first order of business is to know yourself. The only way you can determine if any of the myriad investments out there are right for you is to first understand your own needs. In particular, you want to explore your goals, your time horizon, your income needs, and your risk tolerance.

Goals

If you're reading this book, your primary goal is to have enough assets to generate sufficient income to last the rest of your life. If you are already retired and living off your investments, your goal is to preserve what you have and to make sure your portfolio keeps up with inflation so you can increase your income later on as your expenses rise. If you are still working and saving, your goal is to build your portfolio to the point where you can stop working and start living off your investments. In addition to these major goals, you may also have ancillary goals, such as saving for a vacation or even putting a grandchild through college.

When establishing your goals, it's important to quantify them. How much do you need to have in your bucket before you start siphoning off part of it for income? If you want your retirement fund to generate $30,000 a year and you want it to last at least thirty years, for example, you'll need to start with a $400,000 bucket and earn investment returns of at least 8 percent. Your numbers will be different, of course, depending on your age, your life expectancy, your income needs, your risk tolerance, and your assumed rate of return. You can determine your particular needs by either purchasing a financial software program such as Quicken or sitting down with a financial advisor who can quantify your goals.

Time Horizon

When you want your goal(s) to be achieved will dictate how aggressive or conservative you need to be in your investment strategy. A 60-year-old working person who has very little saved will pursue a very different strategy from a 70-year-old retiree with $1 million in the bucket. Your time horizon will determine how much, if any, you still need to save. It will also determine how liquid your investments need to be and how much volatility you can tolerate. For example, if you are planning to start drawing income next year, you will want to have some of your funds in vehicles that are readily convertible into cash, in order to avoid the risk that they will be down in value at the time you need to liquidate.

But just because you want to start drawing income in a year or two doesn't mean your whole portfolio needs to be liquid. Your real time horizon is the rest of your life. This means you will want to establish different time horizons for portions of your portfolio. For example, you may want to keep enough liquid—either in a money market fund or short-term bond fund—to provide you with income over the next three to five years. Any amount you won't be needing within five years can be invested for growth in a combination of stocks and longer-term bonds or stock and bond mutual funds. This strategy will allow you to rest easy during periods of market volatility because you'll know that, for at least the next five years, your expenses are covered. You won't worry when you see the long-term portion of your portfolio rise and fall in value because you know it goes with the territory of investing for growth.

Income Needs

When you're investing for income, you obviously have to know what your income needs are. That's what this book is all about:

estimating your expenses during retirement, figuring out what sources of income are available to you—Social Security, pension, postretirement salary, and others—and making the arrangements you need to make in order to live comfortably for the rest of your life. Some of your income sources are relatively fixed, such as Social Security and monthly pension. Others are variable, such as income from work (you may decide to work for a few years and then stop) and income from your investment portfolio. Not to beat a dead horse here, but the more you save, and the more your investments earn, the more income you will be able to draw from your investment portfolio when you need it.

The trap we want to caution you from getting into as you think about investment income is focusing exclusively on so-called income-oriented investments. Just because you will be drawing income from your portfolio does not mean you should invest it all in fixed-income securities. Capital gains can be a significant part of your investment returns, even though they can't be predicted in advance.

Now, when you get to step 2, you will see that you may very well want to invest part of the long-term portion of your portfolio in fixed-income securities. But there's a different reason for doing that, and it has nothing to do with your current income needs. We'll get to that in a minute. For now, just remember those poor retirees of the 1970s, who thought the only way to get investment income was to live off the interest and keep the principal intact. For some people, this new model of investing for income may require a change in thinking about the definitions of "income," "growth," and "safety" as they apply to investments.

Risk Tolerance

One aspect of your risk tolerance is how far your stomach goes up and down as your portfolio rises and falls. The emotional aspect of risk is a very real consideration, and the best way to deal with it is through knowledge. The most uninformed people view risk as an all-or-nothing proposition. They think their money is either safe or it's not . . . that they'll either keep it all or lose it all . . . that banks are safe and stocks are not. This is typical thinking among people who view investments from afar and don't understand the nuances that make investments behave as they do. Investments entail different kinds and degrees of risk, and when you understand the forces that cause the price of a particular security to move up and down, you can decide for yourself if the risk is worth it. This is one good reason for letting professional portfolio managers handle your investments. Professionals are experienced at evaluating risk factors because they do it every day.

At the same time, it's important to understand that risk tolerance is about more than emotion. It's also a matter of dollars and cents. If you are getting a late start in planning for retirement, you may need to take more risk than you feel totally comfortable with in order to have a chance at having enough income to last the rest of your life. On the other hand, if you have plenty of money and are not in danger of outliving your savings, there's no reason to take any more risk than you need to. All emotion aside, your real risk tolerance has to do with your age, your life expectancy, the amount of money in your retirement bucket, and the amount of income you'll be siphoning off. If all of these factors indicate that your investment portfolio needs to earn, say, 12 percent in order to be set for life, you will indeed need to take some risk, whether you like it or not. If all you need to earn is 3 percent or 4 percent to keep up with inflation (plus a little more for taxes), then you can avoid the thrills of the stock market and keep your money in Treasury bills.

STEP 2: DEVELOP AN ASSET ALLOCATION PLAN

The next step is to decide where to invest your money. Now, we're not talking about specific investments yet. Rather, we're talking about broad asset classes like stocks, bonds, and cash equivalents, perhaps even real estate or gold. The purpose of placing your money in more than one asset category is to "diversify away" some of the investment risk. One way to understand the concept of diversification is to look at its opposite: concentration. If you put all of your money into one asset and something goes wrong, you have no safety net to protect even part of your portfolio. The most dramatic example of this would be putting your entire life savings into a penny stock or some other risky deal that could go to zero. A less dramatic example is what the retirees of the 1970s did when they put all of their money into CDs and money market funds. Even though their principal was not technically at risk, in effect it was, because they had to tap into it to make up for their loss of income. That experience taught investors everywhere that no matter how seemingly risk-free an investment may be, it's never a good idea to put all your eggs in one basket, even if you watch the basket, because forces beyond your control could come along and knock it out of your hands.

It's those forces beyond your control that you are thinking about when you establish your asset allocation plan. At this writing, the economy is strong (but not too strong), inflation is low, and interest rates are low. In short, conditions are ideal for investing in stocks. But because these circumstances could change at any time without warning, we don't want to put all of our money in stocks. So we'll put some money in bonds, which are more predictable investments because they pay a specified interest rate and will mature at some point in the future, giving us our original principal back. If we really want to cover our bases, we'll contemplate the possibility of inflation going back up into double digits as it did in the late 1970s and early 1980s, and buy gold. Gold is the classic inflation hedge, and its price tends to move opposite to stocks and bonds. Real estate is another inflation hedge. So if interest rates and inflation should go up, our stocks and bonds will probably decline in value, but our gold and real estate will likely appreciate. One scenario that few people have contemplated but that theoretically could happen is deflation. That's where prices are falling and the economy is contracting. Deflation would be bad news for stocks and gold but good news for bonds and cash.

We don't want to make this whole thing more complicated than it needs to be. If you own your home or other collectibles, such as jewelry or artwork, you already have a hedge against inflation, so we're not going to figure gold or any other inflation hedge into our discussion here. Instead, we're going to focus on the classic asset allocation plan that utilizes stocks, bonds, and cash to give you a well-rounded portfolio offering a mix of income, growth, and relative stability. Remember now, when doing your asset allocation plan you are working with all of your investable assets, including IRAs, 401(k)s, and everything else, even though the assets may be divided among separate accounts.

Level-1 Divide: Stocks, Bonds, and Cash

Starting with the cash portion, you'll want to keep emergency funds plus any money you know you'll be needing within the next three to five years in an account that you can get at easily and that has no danger of losing its value. Examples of cash equivalents include money market funds, savings accounts, and three- or six-month Treasury bills. Also included in the cash category would be any investable funds that eventually will find their way into stocks or bonds but that you are not ready to invest yet, either because you are pursuing a strategy of dollar-cost averaging (covered later in this chapter) or you feel nervous about the markets and think stock and bond prices will go a little lower before you decide to invest. Cash equivalents are not usually a good long-term investment in their own right, because returns tend to track the inflation rate and offer no opportunity for growth. They are excellent for liquidity, however, which is necessary when you want to buy stuff.

The remaining portion of your portfolio will be divided between stocks and bonds. When making this decision, keep in mind the main difference between the two: Under normal circumstances, stocks offer greater opportunity for growth but are more volatile; bonds are more stable but offer lower returns. To put it simply, stocks are for growth, bonds are for stability. So going back to your risk tolerance and time horizon, and taking into account your goals and income needs, you decide how much to invest in stocks and bonds respectively.

One rule of thumb, which we don't agree with but which

you may have heard, is to subtract your age from one hundred and invest that amount in stocks. So if you're sixty years old, you'd invest 40 percent of your portfolio in stocks. While the concept of lowering your risk exposure as you get older is a good one, we think the formula is too simplistic and too conservative for most people. A sixty-year-old has a good chance of living another twenty-five or thirty years. Her income needs could more than double over that time, so it is essential that her portfolio keep growing the whole time she is drawing income from it. Since stocks have historically had a better record of staying ahead of inflation, it may be smarter to put 60 or 70 percent into stocks instead.

Level-2 Divide: Stocks and Bonds

Stocks: Small vs. Large, Domestic vs. International, Growth vs. Value

Now that you know what percentage of your portfolio to put into stocks, you can fine-tune your portfolio even further by diversifying among small companies vs. large companies, domestic stocks vs. international stocks, and growth stocks vs. value stocks. Each layer of diversification adds an extra layer of protection by increasing the likelihood that if one class of securities is going down, the other is either going up or staying flat. Generally, small stocks offer greater appreciation potential—and greater volatility—than large stocks. Domestic stocks reflect the U.S. economy, while international stocks reflect the conditions of economies around the globe. Growth stocks offer more appreciation potential but carry more risk, while value stocks tend to have more stable prices but limited upside potential.

Bonds: Long vs. Short, High Quality vs. High Yield

A bond that is set to mature in five years will have a lower yield than a bond of similar quality that matures in thirty years. However, its price will be more stable, and if you think you may need to sell the bond before maturity, that could be an important consideration. A bond with a C rating will offer a higher yield than a bond with a AA rating, but you run the risk of not getting your principal back. There are many ways to slice up the bond portion of your portfolio to maximize yield and minimize risk according to your exact needs and preferences. Since bonds are very complicated and difficult to access in the marketplace (it's virtually impossible for investors to buy individual bonds on their own), most people invest in bonds through mutual funds. Your level-2 diversification decisions will impact which mutual funds you buy. Try to get a mix of short and long bonds, high-quality and high-yield bonds, so you'll be adequately diversified.

Level-3 Divide: Stocks into Sectors

For even further diversification, you can divide the stock portion of your portfolio into industry sectors, putting X percent into technology stocks, X percent into manufacturing stocks, X percent into financial service companies, X percent into utilities, and so on. The reasoning behind this type of allocation is that the various sectors perform differently depending on economic conditions and other circumstances. To ensure broad diversification across all sectors of the economy, you can divide your portfolio evenly among the different industries. Or, if you want to place bets on certain sectors, you can intentionally overweight those sectors based on your outlook for the respective industries. Professional money managers call this a "top-down" approach, first choosing the sectors and then selecting the individual securities within those sectors.

STEP 3: CHOOSE SPECIFIC INVESTMENTS

We know that many investors jump right in with step 3, picking mutual funds or stocks without first having analyzed their needs or developed an asset allocation plan as suggested in steps 1 and 2. If you're one of those people, you have found that it is indeed possible—even easy—to do so. You get a stock tip from a friend or buy a mutual fund off one of the personal finance magazines' top-performing lists, and everything is fine . . . until the stock goes down or the mutual fund drops off the best-performing list. Then you don't know what to do, because the people who told you to buy are never around to tell you when to sell. So you end up with a mish-mash of investments and no plan for managing them.

The asset allocation plan you developed in step 2 will serve as your framework for choosing specific investments in step 3. So instead of starting with the specific investment (the "bottom-up" approach), you start with the asset class, say stocks. Then you narrow it down to, say, large-company stocks. At that point you can buy a mutual fund that invests in large-company stocks, in which case you do not need to diversify further by sector because the mutual fund does it for you. (If you want to know how a particular fund allocates the portfolio across sectors, you can get a copy of the fund's most recent annual or quarterly report, which will list all the stocks in the fund's portfolio as of a specific date.) If you want to buy individual stocks instead of mutual funds, you would further narrow your search by industry and then by individual company. This top-down method ensures that you will have a broad cross-section of securities in your portfolio—regardless of whether you invest in mutual funds or individual stocks.

In fact, when you begin step 3, you may be wondering whether to invest in mutual funds or individual stocks and bonds. The answer depends in part on how much you're investing. It's hard to get adequate diversification in individual securities if you're investing less than $100,000, and you really should have considerably more. If you do decide to invest in individual stocks and bonds, be prepared to do lots of homework and plan to devote several hours a week to managing your portfolio. If you lack the time or inclination to choose individual securities, you can buy a selection of mutual funds based on your asset allocation plan from step 2. Another advantage to owning mutual funds is that they provide a convenient way to reinvest your earnings so your money can compound.

STEP 4: MONITOR AND MANAGE YOUR PORTFOLIO

In some ways, acquiring the investments is the easy part. It's the ongoing managing that either throws people for a loop or causes them to lose interest. Investors who watch the nightly financial news and check the stock or mutual fund tables in the newspaper every day are in danger of being swayed by short-term market events. Those who get bored with financial matters once their portfolio is in place are in danger of letting it get out of control. Fortunately, there's a happy medium. You'll want to check your portfolio often enough to keep tabs on it but not so often that the daily ups and downs make you crazy.

Quarterly Investment Check

At the end of each quarter, you should do a formal check of your entire portfolio by gathering together all of your account statements and seeing where you stand. This quarterly investment check probably will not require any action on your part, but it's a good way to review what happened over the quarter and remind you of what you own.

Annual Portfolio Review and Rebalancing

Once a year, preferably after you have received all of your year-end statements, you'll want to sit down and carefully analyze your portfolio. Note all of the activity that has taken place over the year. Add up the value of your investments and compare the total to last year's balance. Adjusting for additions and withdrawals, are you ahead or behind? By how much? Compare your actual investment returns to your expected investment returns as defined in step 1. Were you hoping for 10 percent but ended up with 8 percent? There's no reason to panic—you could easily make it up next year—but you should always be aware of where you stand compared to where you want to be.

Also see if your asset allocation has changed significantly. If so, you'll need to rebalance your portfolio. Here's how that works. Let's say your asset allocation plan calls for 70 percent stocks and 30 percent bonds and that you start the year with a $100,000 portfolio, $70,000 in stocks and $30,000 in bonds. Let's say at the end of the year your stocks are worth $90,000 and your bonds are worth $33,000. To find out your current allocation, you divide the value of the stocks by the value of the total portfolio—$90,000 ÷ $123,000—and discover that stocks now comprise 75 percent of your portfolio. To restore your original allocation, you would need to have $86,100 in stocks ($123,000 × 70%) and $36,900 in bonds ($123,000 × 30%), so you would sell some of your stocks and put the proceeds into bonds. How often should you rebalance? We recommend doing it once a year, or whenever your allocation becomes skewed by 5 percent or more.

STRATEGIES FOR TAX-ADVANTAGED INVESTING

As noted earlier, the basic investment strategy just outlined applies to both taxable and nontaxable accounts. At steps 3 and 4—after your basic asset allocation plan has been established— you will want to consider the different types of accounts you have and whether you should apply any special tax-saving strategies to the taxable accounts. Here are the steps for doing that:

Step 1: Identify taxable accounts. As you know, retirement accounts are not taxable until the money is withdrawn. So you can move money around all you want within IRAs, 401(k)s, "Keogh" plans, and any other qualified retirement plans you have without worrying about taxes. Earnings on your personal investment funds will, however, be subject to annual income tax. So the first step is to identify those taxable accounts.

Step 2: Determine your tax bracket. If you need to, see Chapter 11 for basic information on taxes. To find out your tax bracket, look at last year's tax return, see what number appears on Line 38, Taxable Income, and check the latest IRS tables to see what tax bracket you are in. If you expect this year's income to be significantly different from last year's, factor in the difference. Don't forget to add in your state tax bracket.

Step 3: If your federal tax bracket is 28 percent or higher, look for tax-saving investment strategies such as the following:

- **Tax-deferred annuities** act like mutual funds, but the investment earnings are not taxed until the funds are taken out of the account, similar to the way IRAs work.

- **Municipal bonds** pay tax-free interest and may be suitable for the bond portion of your portfolio. (Tax-free mutual funds are an easy way to invest in municipal bonds.)

- **Tax-advantaged mutual funds** pay attention to the timing of stock and bond purchases and sales and use other sophisticated strategies in order to minimize tax consequences for shareholders.

- **A buy-and-hold strategy** applied to stocks can postpone capital gains to a later tax year.

Step 4: As a rule of thumb for ongoing investing, if you are comparing two investments with different tax consequences, always place the one with the higher tax consequences into your retirement account.

STRATEGIES FOR ONGOING INVESTING

Dollar-cost averaging is a fancy name for investing that is done on a regular, periodic basis. The theory behind it is that by investing equal amounts at regular intervals, you take advantage of price fluctuations to acquire more shares when prices are down and fewer shares when prices are up. In reality, you will probably invest as the money becomes available, generally when you get paid. So rather than being concerned about whether it's the right time to invest, you just keep making your automatic investments, regardless of whether prices are going up or down. As long as you stick to the plan, and as long as the overall price trend is up, you will make money. Some mutual funds offer automatic investment programs that transfer a specified amount directly from your checking account. If you find your resolve weakening when the markets are being volatile, this may be the way to go.

Another way to use dollar-cost averaging is when you have a large lump sum and are nervous about jumping into the stock and bond markets all at once. By investing portions of the money at regular intervals, you can avoid being paralyzed with fear. Take it from us, nobody ever knows if it's the right time to invest. If you hold it all in cash until a better time comes along, that time will never come. Dollar-cost averaging allows you to ease into the markets in a sensible, disciplined manner.

KEEPING YOUR RETIREMENT BUCKET FULL WHILE DRAWING THE INCOME YOU NEED

The old-fashioned way of investing for retirement was to concentrate on growth investments while you were working and then shift everything over to income investments on the day you retired. But now that we know about inflation and the hazards of trying to live on a fixed income for fifteen or twenty or thirty years, we know that retirement savings must keep growing throughout a retiree's lifetime. So the day you punch a hole in your retirement bucket and start siphoning off income will not necessarily mark a big change in your investment strategy. You will keep filling the bucket from the top—with investment earnings alone if your own contributions stop—while you gradually draw income off the bottom.

Here's an example of how that works. Let's say you retire at age sixty-five and have $400,000 in your retirement bucket, which is earning an average of 10 percent per year. You start collecting $15,000 a year in Social Security benefits and get a part-time job making $12,000 a year. That's a total of $27,000. Let's say you need a total income of $50,000. To make up the difference, you'd set up a systematic withdrawal program to take $23,000 out of your $400,000 retirement bucket as shown in Table 6.1.

TABLE **6.1**   **KEEPING YOUR RETIREMENT BUCKET**
GROWING WHILE TAKING THE
INCOME YOU NEED

$400,000—Retirement—age 65
+40,000—Investment earnings 1st year
−23,000—Withdrawal 1st year

$417,000—End of year 1
+41,700—Investment earnings 2nd year
−23,000—Withdrawal 2nd year

$435,700—End of year 2
+43,570—Investment earnings 3rd year
−23,000—Withdrawal 3rd year

$456,270—End of year 3
+45,627—Investment earnings 4th year
−23,000—Withdrawal 4th year

$478,897—End of year 4
+47,890—Investment earnings 5th year
−23,000—Withdrawal 5th year

$503,787—End of year 5—age 70
+50,379—Investment earnings 6th year
−34,000—Withdrawal 6th year

$520,166—End of year 6
+52,017—Investment earnings 7th year
−34,000—Withdrawal 7th year

$538,183—End of year 7
+53,818—Investment earnings 8th year
−34,000—Withdrawal 8th year

$558,001—End of year 8
+55,800—Investment earnings 9th year
−34,000—Withdrawal 9th year

$579,801—End of year 9
  +57,980—Investment earnings 10th year
  −34,000—Withdrawal 10th year

$603,781—End of year 10—age 75
  +64,378—Investment earnings 11th year
  −40,000—Withdrawal 11th year

$624,159—End of year 11
  +62,416—Investment earnings 12th year
  −40,000—Withdrawal 12th year

$646,575—End of year 12
  + 64,658—Investment earnings 13th year
  −40,000—Withdrawal 13th year

$671,233—End of year 13
  +67,123—Investment earnings 14th year
  −40,000—Withdrawal 14th year

$695,891—End of year 14
  +69,589—Investment earnings 15th year
  −40,000—Withdrawal 15th year

$735,480—End of year 15—age 80

If we call your first year of retirement "year 1," you see from the table that in the first year, you're earning $40,000 in investment returns and siphoning off $23,000 in income. That makes your retirement bucket worth $417,000 at the end of year 1. You keep doing this for five years and then decide to give yourself a cost-of-living raise. At the same time, you decide to cut back your hours and earn $6,000 a year in wages instead of $12,000. So you start taking out $34,000, while leaving the rest to grow. Five years later, you stop working altogether, give yourself another cost-of-living raise, and start taking out $40,000. As you can see, the bucket is not in danger of becoming empty—in fact, it's growing! Five years later, you're 80 years old and on your way to becoming a millionaire. The key to success here is to make sure your portfolio is growing faster than you are depleting it.

In this example, the portfolio must earn at least 10 percent in order for the withdrawal program to work. Your situation may be different. If your bucket is already pretty full, you won't need to earn so much. If you want to take out more income than we used in this example, you may need to earn more. Try not to make your assumptions too aggressive, however, because the more you hope to earn, the more risk you'll have to take, and you don't want to be losing money when you're 70 or 80 years old and have no means to make it back.

Table 6.2 shows how many years your money will last if you need to take out more than your investment portfolio is earning. Your goal, if possible, is to always make sure your investment portfolio is earning at least as much as you are taking out. However, that may not be possible, especially in your later years. To see how long your portfolio will last at various returns and withdrawal rates, refer to the table. Across the top are the rates of return. Down the side are the withdrawal amounts. For example, if your retirement savings are earning 8 percent and you are withdrawing 10 percent, your money will last twenty years. If you withdraw 9 percent, your money will last twenty-eight years. Please note that this table does not factor taxes or inflation into the mix. Therefore, it should be used as a guide only, to give you some idea of how much you can withdraw and how long your money may be expected to last. And, of course, nobody can predict with certainty what your investment returns will be in the future. You will still need to keep your eye on the bucket to make sure you are not draining it too fast.

STRATEGIES FOR DRAWING INCOME

The mechanics of drawing income from your retirement accounts will depend on where the accounts are and how the money is invested. Again, you will want to look at all of your accounts in their entirety when planning your withdrawal strategy. You'll want to preserve your balance of stocks and bonds as much as possible, and you'll also need to consider the tax consequences of your withdrawals.

TABLE **6.2**   **HOW LONG YOUR PORTFOLIO WILL LAST IF YOUR RATE OF WITHDRAWAL EXCEEDS YOUR RATE OF RETURN**

Average Annual Rate of Return on Your Investment

RATE OF ANNUAL WITHDRAWAL (%)	%								
	1	2	3	4	5	6	7	8	9
10	10	11	12	13	14	15	17	20	26
9	11	12	13	14	16	18	22	28	
8	13	14	15	17	20	23	30		
7	15	16	18	21	25	33			
6	18	20	23	28	36				
5	22	25	31	41					
4	28	35	46						
3	40	55							
2	69								

NUMBER OF YEARS YOUR MONEY WILL LAST

In general, it's wise to draw from regular taxable accounts first and leave IRAs and other retirement plans alone so you can let tax-deferred earnings grow as long as possible. As you approach retirement (or whatever we're calling the day you start taking income from your investments), think about which account(s) you'll draw from first and start preparing for those withdrawals.

There are a couple of ways you can go about this. One way is to liquidate enough stocks and bonds to provide three to five years' worth of income and place the proceeds in a money market fund. Then you write yourself a check every month, or whenever you need funds. This strategy reduces the risk that you'll have to liquidate investments at a bad time in order to take the income you need. However, it does deprive you of the growth and income that those stocks and bonds might have provided over the next three to five years.

Another way to do it—and this works best if you have your money invested in mutual funds—is to set up a systematic withdrawal plan whereby the mutual fund liquidates enough shares to provide you with a set amount of income every month. Most mutual funds will do this, and you can even have the funds automatically deposited to your checking account if you want to save a trip to the bank.

PART
THREE

Other Sources of Income During Retirement

CHAPTER SEVEN

Social Security

Sure, I'm for helping the elderly.
I'm going to be old myself someday.

—Lillian Carter (in her 80s)

Keeping up with Social Security is like going after a moving target. The program will necessarily undergo major changes to keep from going broke before the last of the baby boomers retire, but at this point it's anyone's guess what those changes will be. So when incorporating Social Security into your financial plan, it's best to focus on the program as it exists today and as it applies to you, not what it might be in the future. You may want to be mindful of the various proposals and how they may affect you, but until an amendment is signed into law, remember that any particular proposal is conjecture and nothing more. Also keep in mind that the older you are now, the less likely Social Security will change substantially for you. As much as the system needs fixing, nobody wants to let down a generation of retirees who've been counting on the system to support them in their old age.

THE ORIGINAL INTENT
OF SOCIAL SECURITY

The Social Security system has been a godsend to millions of people. When it was first signed into law by President Franklin Delano Roosevelt on August 14, 1935, it was hailed as the solution to poverty and destitution in old age. As part of the New Deal, Social Security addressed a relatively new problem ushered in by the industrial revolution: People could no longer count on their extended family for support because they had moved away from the farms and into the cities. So when the streets became populated with elderly people looking for a handout in the midst of the Great Depression, Social Security was created to save people from the "hazards and vicissitudes of life."

The program we all recognize today as Social Security was actually part of a larger program that included welfare for the poor. Roosevelt's idea was to have Title I, the welfare part, support people in the early years of the program until the contributory system became self-sustaining. On January 31, 1940, the contributory system issued its first monthly retirement check in the amount of $22.54 to Ida May Fuller of Ludlow, Vermont. Miss Fuller collected a total of $22,000 over her thirty-five years as a beneficiary before her death in 1975 at the age of 100. In the sixty-plus years that the Social Security system has been operating, more than $4.1 trillion has been paid out in benefits.

Because most working people pay into the system through paycheck deductions, it's easy to think of Social Security as an entitlement program. You expect to get back what you paid in. But at this point in the system's history, it may be helpful to remember that Social Security was enacted as part of a general welfare program. It was designed to eradicate widespread poverty by giving more help to those who need it. Even the contributory part has always skewed benefits in favor of lower-income people by replacing a larger percentage of their earnings. Thinking of Social Security in this way may help succeeding generations of workers become less reliant on the system for the majority of their retirement income, which Social Security was never designed to provide anyway.

How Social Security works

Social Security is a gigantic trust fund that most working people pay into (some government employees and railroad workers are excluded) through automatic paycheck deductions. As the money flows into the trust fund, it is immediately paid out to current retirees. Contrary to what some people think, each worker's contribution is not held in a separate account to be collected later by that worker. Instead, all the contributions are thrown into one huge pot from which current benefits are paid. If more money is taken in than paid out—which is occurring now that baby boomers are in the workforce in full swing—the excess is invested in U.S. government securities that pay interest at prevailing rates. In order for the system to keep working, it must remain in *actuarial balance*. This means that future benefits must be accurately forecasted and enough Social Security taxes collected to cover them. Currently the system is not in actuarial balance because starting around 2012, far more people (read: baby boomers) will be collecting benefits than will be paying in. Various proposals have been raised to address this problem, and by the time you read this, the solution may be under way.

If you are currently working, the amount deducted from your paycheck is 7.65 percent of your gross salary up to a limit set by law ($72,600 in 1999). Your employer contributes an equal amount for a total of 15.3 percent. If you are self-employed, you pay the entire 15.3 percent yourself. So if you earned the wage limit of $72,600 in 1999, a total of $11,108 was paid into Social Security by you and/or your employer (15.3% of $72,600 = $11,108). Over the years, a total of more than $4.5 trillion has been paid into the Social Security system.

Qualifying for benefits

Social Security retirement benefits are based on your work history (or your spouse's work history if your own work history is limited). While you are working, your wages are posted to your Social Security record. These wages determine two things: (1) whether you will be eligible for Social Security retirement benefits in the first place, and (2) how much your monthly check will be when you eventually begin drawing benefits.

To get basic eligibility, you need forty *earnings credits.* You get one earnings credit for each $740 in wages, and you can earn a maximum of four credits per year (the amount required for each earnings credit rises every year; $740 was the amount in 1999). If you earn more than $2,960 in a year ($740 × 4), you do not receive more credits—you can only receive four earnings credits a year. Earnings credits are used to determine basic eligibility only, and all you need are 40 of them to qualify. Generally, this means you must work for at least ten years, not necessarily all in one stretch. This can be important for people who have taken breaks to raise children or pursue other interests and who may find themselves a few credits shy of the required forty; there may still be time to go back to work and earn more credits to attain basic eligibility. (Note: If you were born in 1928 you need 39 credits; if you were born in 1927 you need 38; and on down to 35 credits if you were born in 1924.)

The second part of the equation, how much your monthly check will be when you eventually begin drawing benefits, is much more complicated. The easiest way to find out is to call the Social Security Administration at 800-772-1213 and ask for a Personal Earnings and Benefit Statement (PEBS). It's free, and in addition to giving you an estimate of your benefits, it will allow you to verify that all of your earnings have been properly posted to your account so you can resolve any discrepancies now.

But even if you plan to get a personalized estimate of your benefits, it's also a good idea to understand how Social Security benefits are calculated so you can see if there's anything you can to do increase your benefits. The calculations are complicated, and you don't even want to know all the actuarial assumptions that go into them, but knowing the basic steps can be helpful. First, the Social Security Administration determines how many years of earnings will be used as a base. Thirty-five years of earnings are considered for everyone born after 1928, fewer for people born in 1928 or earlier. If you did not work a total of thirty-five years, those missing years will be filled in with a "zero" when calculating your average earnings. If you worked more than thirty-five years, your highest earning years will be used. Next, your actual earnings are adjusted, or "indexed," to account for wage inflation over the years and then averaged to arrive at your *average indexed monthly earnings* (AIME). Finally, a formula is applied to your AIME to arrive at your *primary insurance amount* (PIA). This is the amount you will receive if you begin drawing benefits at *full retirement age*. Full retirement age used to be sixty-five for everyone, but it's been pushed back due to longer life expectancies and the worry that those baby boomers will decimate the trust fund before their kids can get at it. Full retirement age now depends on when you were born and is explained in Table 7.1.

TABLE **7.1**   AGE WHEN YOU ARE ELIGIBLE TO RECEIVE FULL SOCIAL SECURITY BENEFITS

YEAR OF BIRTH	FULL RETIREMENT AGE
1937 OR EARLIER	65
1938	65 and 2 months
1939	65 and 4 months
1940	65 and 6 months
1941	65 and 8 months
1942	65 and 10 months
1943–1954	66
1955	66 and 2 months
1956	66 and 4 months
1957	66 and 6 months
1958	66 and 8 months
1959	66 and 10 months
1960 AND LATER	67

If you had what the Social Security Administration considered *average earnings* in 1997, or about $25,000, your benefit would be calculated to replace about 42 percent of your earnings. If your earnings were higher than the average, the replacement percentage would be lower, but the dollar amount would be higher. To get an idea of what your benefits might be, see Table 7.2, which uses the latest numbers available from the Social Security Administration.

TABLE 7.2 LIKELY SOCIAL SECURITY BENEFITS

YOUR AGE IN 1997	YOUR EARNINGS IN 1996	BENEFITS FOR YOU	BENEFITS FOR YOU AND YOUR SPOUSE*
45	$20,000	$ 797	$1,195
	30,000	1,063	1,594
	40,000	1,229	1,843
	50,000	1,354	2,031
	62,700 or more	1,519	2,278
55	20,000	797	1,195
	30,000	1,063	1,594
	40,000	1,226	1,839
	50,000	1,327	1,990
	62,700 or more	1,435	2,152
65	20,000	805	1,207
	30,000	1,074	1,611
	40,000	1,205	1,272
	50,000	1,272	1,908
	62,700 or more	1,326	1,989

* Your spouse has the choice of qualifying under your work history or his or her own, whichever will result in higher benefits.

Factors that can raise or lower Social Security benefits

Once the basic benefit has been calculated, several things can happen to raise or lower it.

Early Retirement

You don't have to wait until you've reached full retirement age to begin collecting Social Security benefits. Regardless of when you were born, you can apply for benefits as early as age 62. But it may end up costing you. First, your average earnings will probably be lower because you won't have the earnings of later years to boost the average. Second, each benefit check will be lower to make up for the fact that you'll be receiving more checks over your lifetime. If your full retirement age is 65, the reduction for starting Social Security at age 62 is about 20 percent; at age 63, it's about 13⅓ percent; at age 64, it's about 6⅔ percent. So if your primary insurance amount (the amount you would normally collect at full retirement age) is, say, $1,200, you would receive about $960 per month if you were to begin collecting at age 62.

In theory, it's all supposed to balance out. Whether you retire at age 62 or age 65, the system is designed to provide the same total dollars over your lifetime—assuming you live the exact number of years the actuarial tables say you're expected to live. And this is where the planning comes in. If you think you'll live longer than the Social Security people think you will, you're better off waiting until age 65 (or later) to begin collecting benefits. That's because the benefit reduction that occurs when you take early retirement is permanent—your check starts out lower and stays lower for the rest of your life. The breakeven age is about 77. If you live longer than that, you will end up collecting more total benefits over your lifetime if you wait until age 65 to start. And the longer you live past age 77, the greater the advantage will be. So check out your gene pool and see how long your parents and grandparents lived. Also take a look at your lifestyle and general health to get an idea of how long you may be expected to live. In any case, it's just good planning to assume you'll live a long time—because if you plan for a short life and you end up outliving your money, you're . . . well, dead.

There are a couple of circumstances under which it may make sense to apply for benefits early. One is when a spouse wants to receive benefits based on her own work history before switching over to the higher spousal benefit. Let's say the husband had high earnings over his lifetime, and the wife had low earnings. (Sorry for the stereotype, but that's usually the way it works.) Due to the husband's higher earnings, the wife would normally receive more by electing to take her spousal benefit instead of opting for a benefit based on her own work history. However, she may not begin collecting her spousal benefit until her husband applies for benefits. If he delays the start of benefits, she can go ahead and apply at age 62 under her own work record. Then when her husband applies, her benefits will automatically be bumped up. This will allow her to pocket a few years worth of benefits before the husband's benefits start. Widows and widowers can use a similar strategy. But in this case it works if your own benefits would be higher than your widow(er)'s benefits. You can apply for widow(er)'s benefits as early as age 60, then when you turn 62 or 65 you can apply for benefits based on your own work history and bump up the benefits. The rules vary depending on the situation, so be sure to talk to the Social Security people about the options available to you.

The other circumstance under which it might make sense to apply for Social Security before age 65 is if you retire early and do not wish to touch any money you have growing in tax-deferred accounts such as IRAs. (More on these in Chapter 7.) If you're going to need income and wish to leave your tax-sheltered funds undisturbed so they can grow as rapidly as possible until the mandatory distribution laws take effect at age 70½, Social Security—even at the reduced amount—may be an important source of income for you. The tax-deferred compounding in the IRA may even make up for the reduced lifetime benefit from Social Security, depending on your life expectancy and how much you have in the IRA.

LATER RETIREMENT

What if you're not ready to retire at 65? Is there any advantage to waiting to collect Social Security? Yes. First, the longer you work, the higher your average earnings are likely to be. (Remember that zero- or low-earning years are replaced with high-earning years when your benefits are calculated, so the longer you prolong your peak earning years, the higher your average will be).

Second, the longer you wait to collect Social Security—up to age 70—the higher your monthly check will be. For each year after normal retirement age that you delay collecting benefits, the amount goes up by anywhere from 3 to 8 percent a year (compounded) depending on when you were born. Table 7.3 shows the benefit increases by year of birth.

TABLE **7.3** INCREASES FOR DELAYED RETIREMENT

YEAR OF BIRTH	YEARLY RATE OF INCREASE (%)
1917–1924	3
1924–1926	3.5
1927–1928	4
1929–1930	4.5
1931–1932	5
1933–1934	5.5
1935–1936	6
1937–1938	6.5
1939–1940	7
1941–1942	7.5
1943 OR LATER	8

So if you were born in 1943 or later and your benefit would normally be $1,200, you could increase it to over $1,700 by waiting until age 70 to begin collecting. In this case, you would need to live at least to age 80 in order for the delay of benefits to provide a higher lifetime total compared to applying for benefits at normal retirement age.

Please note that if you do delay the start of your Social Security benefits, you should still sign up for Medicare at age 65. In some circumstances, medical insurance costs more if you delay applying for it. Please see Chapter 13 for more information on Medicare.

The age at which you begin collecting Social Security benefits is a very personal matter. It's a decision you should weigh carefully after considering your health, your financial situation, your life expectancy, and your feelings about continuing to work. Speaking of which . . .

Working During Retirement

Another thing that can change the amount of your Social Security check is the amount of income you earn if you continue working. This is called the *earnings limitation*, or *retirement test*, and it applies until you reach age 70. If you earn more than the earnings limitation, Social Security will reduce your benefits by a dollar for each $1.00 or $2.00 (depending on your age) over the limit that you earn. For people age 62 through 64, the earnings limitation in 1999 is $9,600 per year. For each $2.00 earned over the limit, $1.00 of Social Security is withheld. So, for example, if you were age 63 and earned $16,000 in 1998, your Social Security would be reduced by $2,940 ($15,000 – $9,600 = $6,400 ÷ 2 = $3,200). That amounts to $267 a month.

Once you reach age 65, the earnings limitation eases up a bit. Between ages 65 and 69 you can earn up to $15,500 (in 1999) with no cut in benefits. If you earn more than that, your benefit is cut by $1.00 for every $3.00 you earn over the limit. So if you earned $16,000 at age 65, your benefit would be reduced by only $166 for the year ($16,000 – $15,500 = $500 ÷ 3 = $166). The earnings limitation is adjusted every year to account for inflation.

After age 70 you are no longer subject to the earnings limitation and can earn as much as you want without it affecting your Social Security benefits. Age 70 is also the magic year that it no longer pays to delay the start of benefits. So once you hit that age, your decisions are pretty much made for you: Start collecting Social Security (if you haven't already done so), and feel free to earn as much income as you want from working. Between the ages of 62 and 69, however, you have some decisions to make. The age at which you decide to apply for benefits will depend on two key factors: (1) how long you think you'll live, and (2) whether you will continue to work and how much income you'll earn. As noted, our recommendation is to assume you'll live a long time. The whole point of financial planning, after all, is to ensure that you'll have enough money to last the rest of your life, and planning for an early death doesn't make much sense. So if you are age 62 through 69, and if your financial situation is such that you can afford to delay taking benefits, consider waiting until age 70 to apply for Social Security. Your lifetime benefit will likely be higher and you won't have to worry about the earnings limitation. Besides, if you wait until age 70 to begin collecting benefits, your benefit may be enough higher—between the bonus for waiting and your higher average earnings—that you won't need to worry about working at all.

What if you are between the ages of 62 and 69 and have already started collecting Social Security benefits? Does it pay to work if you earn more than the earnings limitation? Sorry, but we can't give you a pat answer to this. At first glance it might seem that, of course, it pays to work. Between your earned income and Social Security (even at a reduced amount), you end up with more money. For example, let's say you're 65 and your normal Social Security check (if you didn't work) would be $1,200 a month or $14,400 a year. If you work part time and earn $20,000 a year in salary, your Social Security will be reduced to $12,900. But you'll also have the $20,000 in salary, for a total of $32,900. However, this calculation does not take into account any expenses that may be connected with earning the $20,000. The biggest, of course, is income tax, but there may be other expenses, such as commuting costs or business expenses. By the time you put a pencil to it and see what percentage of the $20,000 you actually get to keep, also taking into account the reduction in Social Security benefits, you may decide it's not worth it to work—especially if the job entails any hassles you'd just soon not put up with.

By the way, the earnings limitation applies to earned income only. It does not apply to pension or IRA distributions, investment income such as dividends or capital gains, or rental income (unless you're in the real estate business). One smart retirement planning strategy is to arrange to have sufficient income from these other sources so you won't have to worry about the Social Security earnings limitation. That's what the next four chapters are about.

COST-OF-LIVING ALLOWANCES (COLAs)

Before 1950, there were no cost-of-living adjustments in the Social Security system. Ida May Fuller, the first Social Security recipient, received $22.54 every month for ten years until 1950, when Congress legislated an increase in benefits, causing her check to go up to $41.30. Between 1950 and 1975, it took an act of Congress each time Social Security benefits needed to be raised. Then in 1975, cost-of-living allowances were built into the system to raise benefits automatically each year based on consumer price increases (see Table 7.4).

Although Social Security COLAs provide you with more income each year to keep up with inflation, do keep in mind our cautionary notes about inflation in Chapter 3. Cost-of-living increases don't do you much good if the things *you* spend money on are going up in price faster than the items used for the Social Security COLA calculation. However, for planning purposes it's nice to know that inflation of some sort is already factored into the Social Security system.

TABLE **7.4**   **SOCIAL SECURITY BENEFIT INCREASES, 1950–1998**

EFFECTIVE DATE	INCREASE (%)	EFFECTIVE DATE	INCREASE (%)
9/50	77.0	6/82	7.4
9/52	12.5	12/83	3.5
9/54	13.0	12/84	3.5
1/59	7.0	12/85	3.1
1/65	7.0	12/86	1.3
2/68	13.0	12/87	4.2
1/70	15.0	12/88	4.0
1/71	10.0	12/89	4.7
9/72	20.0	12/90	5.4
3/74	7.0	12/91	3.7
6/74	11.0	12/92	3.0
6/75	8.0	12/93	2.6
6/76	6.4	12/94	2.8
6/77	5.9	12/95	2.6
6/78	6.5	12/96	2.9
6/79	9.9	12/97	2.1
6/80	14.3	12/98	1.3
6/81	11.2		

PLANNING AHEAD: HOW TO GET THE MOST OUT OF SOCIAL SECURITY

If you are several years away from applying for Social Security benefits, there may be some things you can do now to increase the benefits you will eventually receive.

BOOST YOUR PRERETIREMENT EARNINGS

To get the highest Social Security benefit, your earnings must equal or exceed the Social Security wage base ($72,600 in 1999) every year for thirty-five years. If you spent some time bagging groceries or otherwise failed to "max out on Social Security" during any of your top thirty-five working years, you can replace those lower-earning years with higher-earning ones by moonlighting, starting a part-time business, or asking your boss for a raise. Table 7.5 shows the maximum earnings that will be counted in Social Security benefit calculations for years 1951 through 1999.

If you do not have thirty-five years of work history, keep in mind that every year you did not work counts as a zero in computing your benefits. If your career history is somewhat spotty due to breaks or periods of low-paying jobs, it may be worth postponing retirement in order to gain a few more years of work history and raise your average earnings. If you can't or don't want to stay longer at your regular job, consider switching careers or getting another job in order to boost your earnings. The sacrifice may well be worth it. Remember that Social Security is lifetime income. If you start collecting benefits at 70 and live to age 95, that's twenty-five years of income. If you can raise your benefits by $100 a month, you'll wind up receiving $30,000 more than you otherwise would have, not to mention the extra income you will have received from working, and not counting Social Security cost-of-living increases.

TABLE 7.5 **MAXIMUM EARNINGS COUNTED IN BENEFIT CALCULATIONS**

YEAR	MAXIMUM EARNINGS	YEAR	MAXIMUM EARNINGS
1951	$ 3,600	1976	$15,300
1952	3,600	1977	16,500
1953	3,600	1978	17,700
1954	3,600	1979	22,900
1955	4,200	1980	25,900
1956	4,200	1981	29,700
1957	4,200	1982	32,400
1958	4,200	1983	35,700
1959	4,800	1984	37,800
1960	4,800	1985	39,600
1961	4,800	1986	42,000
1962	4,800	1987	43,800
1963	4,800	1988	45,000
1964	4,800	1989	48,000
1965	4,800	1990	51,300
1966	6,600	1991	53,400
1967	6,600	1992	55,500
1968	7,800	1993	57,600
1969	7,800	1994	60,600
1970	7,800	1995	61,200
1971	7,800	1996	62,700
1972	9,000	1997	65,400
1973	10,800	1998	68,400
1974	13,200	1999	72,600
1975	14,100		

CONSIDER THE CONSEQUENCES OF DIVORCE

As if divorce weren't hard enough, here's another thing to think about: the possibility of receiving Social Security benefits based on your ex-spouse's (or soon-to-be-ex-spouse's) work history. If you have been married to someone with a high earnings record, you may be better off receiving Social Security benefits based on your spouse's income rather than your own. Here are the four tests for qualifying: (1) one-half of your ex-spouse's age-65 benefit is higher than the benefit you would receive based on your own work history; (2) you were married for at least ten years; (3) you've been divorced for at least two years; and (4) you are not married to someone else at the time you start to get the benefit. You can begin receiving checks as soon as both you and your ex are at least 62, even if neither of you is retired. (If you remarry after you start to collect, you lose the ex-spousal benefit.)

Understanding these tests can help in planning. For example, if you're considering getting a divorce after nine years of marriage, it may be worth it to stick it out another year in order to qualify for ex-spousal benefits. Also, you may want to rethink the prospect of remarriage if it will cause you to lose ex-spousal benefits. (Obviously, there's more to think about here than cold financial issues, but our job is to bring these things to your attention.) And by the way, if you've been divorced for years and are not on particularly good terms with your ex-spouse, don't worry about applying for benefits under his or her work record. He/she won't even know you've applied, and it won't affect the amount of your ex-spouse's benefit.

APPLYING FOR BENEFITS

From about age 55 on, you'll want to be in periodic contact with the Social Security people. During your fifties, you'll be verifying your earnings record and getting benefits estimates. As you get into your sixties, you'll be talking to them about how and when to apply for benefits.

To apply, call the Social Security's toll-free number, 1-800-772-1213, or make an appointment to visit any Social Security office to apply in person. Depending on your circumstances, you will need some or all of the following documents:

- Your Social Security number
- Your birth certificate
- Your W-2 forms or self-employment tax return for last year
- Your military discharge papers if you had military service
- Your spouse's birth certificate and Social Security number if he or she is applying for benefits
- Proof of U.S. citizenship (or lawful alien status if you were born outside the United States)
- The name of your bank and your account number so your benefits can be directly deposited into your account.

In one of your planning conversations with the Social Security people, ask about the best time to apply for benefits. It's different for everyone, depending on the age at which you plan to start receiving benefits and the amount of earned income you expect to have during your first year. For example, you can apply for benefits starting in January even though you won't be retiring until later in the year; your first year's benefit may be reduced by the earnings limitation, but you may still end up with more benefits than if you had waited until your actual retirement date to receive your first check. In any case, you need to apply at least three months before the date you want your benefits to start.

CHAPTER EIGHT

Corporate Pensions

*I advise you to go on living solely to enrage
those who are paying your annuities.
It is the only pleasure I have left.*

—Voltaire

I f you think the decision about when to apply for Social Security is a big one, wait till you get to your pension. There are only a couple of decisions you need to make with regard to your pension, but they're doozies. And if you blow it, you could be really, really sorry. But not to worry. We'll tell you some of the things you need to think about when faced with these decisions, and you can always consult a professional advisor when the time comes. The first decision relates to how you want to take your benefits: all at once or in dribs and drabs. Then after you've made that decision, you have to decide whether to roll it over or pay taxes (if you take it all at once), *or* whether to have the dribs and drabs stop when you die or continue on for your surviving spouse or beneficiary.

If you're already lost, don't worry. We'll go back and explain these major pension decisions in a minute. But first, let's assume you're still working for a company that offers a tradi-tional pension plan and that you're just now beginning to pay attention to those annual benefit statements you've been getting the whole time you've been a faithful servant to the company. What once seemed like irrelevant numbers take on a whole new meaning now that you're within a few years of retiring. And since these numbers (or something close to them) may actually appear on a check someday, you'll want to make sure they're right. (By the way, we're talking mainly about traditional defined benefit plans here; if you also have a 401[k] plan, you've probably been keeping close tabs on it and know exactly what it's worth at any given point in time.)

CHECKING YOUR PENSION

Pull out your last benefit statement. Look at it. This may seem really obvious, but is your name spelled right? Is your Social Security number correct? Is your birth date correct? The date you began working? Your age and years of service help determine the amount of your pension, so if these numbers are off, your pension could be off—by a rather large amount. And if your Social Security number is in error, somebody else could be getting credit for all your years of toil. Now's the time to make the corrections, when you're still at the company and in a position to lean on the human resources department. By the way, it's probably too late for this now, but all those pay stubs and W-2 forms that you thought were not needed anymore once each year's taxes were done could help you prove how many hours you worked. Let's hope you won't need them.

What we're getting at here is that sometimes companies make mistakes. An audit conducted by the Pension Benefit Guaranty Corporation in 1997 revealed that 8 percent of employees who got lump sum payouts in 1994–95 didn't get all the money they were entitled to, and about one-third were underpaid by at least $1,000. Other estimates of shortchanged retirees have run as high as 50 percent. It's easy to assume your company's pension benefit calculations are correct when, in fact, the odds of making a mistake are pretty good. For example, in 1997 Ceridian Corp. in Minneapolis settled a class-action lawsuit after it shortchanged retirees to the tune of $51 million because it used an incorrect interest rate to calculate benefits. The miscalculation caused each employee to lose an average of $4,300 in pension benefits.

What can you do to make sure your pension is calculated correctly? The first thing is to verify that all the information about *you* is correct, particularly your years of service, age, and salary. Next, take your pension information to an independent actuary or pension administrator and ask to have the calculations verified. The actuary will need to see your last benefit statement and all the basic information about your plan, such as the summary plan description, latest annual report, and any other disclosure documents you may have received from the company. You should have received these papers already, but you can get copies from your plan administrator or human resources department if you need to. If your company is uncooperative, or you don't want to bother human resources, or you think something fishy may be going on, you can get the summary plan description and latest annual report (Form 5500 Series) from the Department of Labor. Contact the U.S. Department of Labor, PWBA, Public Disclosure Facility, Room N5638, 200 Constitution Avenue, NW, Washington, DC, 20210, (202-219-8771). Expect to pay a reasonable copying charge for the documents. The actuary will charge a professional fee, of course (ask in advance what the charge will be), but it could turn out to be the best money you ever spent. To find an actuary in your area, call the American Society of Pension Actuaries (703-516-9300) or the American Academy of Actuaries (202-223-8196).

One common error relates to the way your pension is integrated with Social Security. Simply stated, a company has the right to reduce your pension by the amount of your expected Social Security benefit. This is becoming a controversial issue because it favors highly paid employees over lower-paid ones. Companies say it's perfectly ethical because it removes Social Security's inherent bias toward lower-income workers and pays the companies back for all the years they paid into the Social

Security system at the same time they were contributing to the pension plan. All controversy aside, if a company subtracts too much from your pension because it miscalculated your Social Security benefit, that's illegal, and you need to have it corrected. Since companies can never know for sure what your earnings history has been, they rely on certain assumptions to estimate your Social Security benefits. But if those assumptions are wrong—say you spent several years out of the workforce to raise a family or worked for a government agency that was exempt from the Social Security system—the company will subtract too much from your pension. To have it corrected, get your actual earnings history from the Social Security Administration (call 800-772-1213), give it to your employer, and ask to have your benefit recalculated. Lower-paid workers and women who have spent time out of the workforce are especially subject to this type of error, so if you fall into one of those categories, watch out for it.

Understanding your pension

Let's assume for the moment that your company has calculated your pension correctly. Does this mean that you are entitled to the exact benefit indicated on your benefit statement? Not necessarily. In fact, probably not. The assumptions used in the estimates may be very different from your actual circumstances when you eventually retire.

In the most common form of pension, the size of your eventual benefit depends on your age at retirement, how much you earn, how long you work for the company, and the benefit formula built into the plan. A typical formula calculates the size of your benefit by multiplying a percentage (say, 1 to 2 percent) of your final pay—or more precisely, of the average of your last three to five years' pay by the number of years you worked for the firm. Regardless of when you actually leave work, you can't start collecting that benefit until you reach the plan's standard retirement age, typically 60 to 65, unless you qualify for early retirement. That's usually decided by some combination of age and years of service.

So if your benefit estimate is based on a retirement age of 65 and assumes you'll take your pension in a monthly check over your lifetime only (this is called a single-life annuity), your actual benefit could be quite different from the estimate if you decide to retire earlier than age 65, or if you want the checks to go to your spouse or other beneficiary after you're gone (a joint-and-survivor annuity). In other words, if you do not fit the mold of the hypothetical retiree, your benefit could be very different from what you expected.

What can you do to make sure you get the maximum benefit you're entitled to? *Don't leave the company!* The last thing you want to do at this stage is get all in a huff about something and storm out the door yelling "I quit." Although you may get some kind of pension, it will be a pittance compared to what you would get if you waited until normal retirement age. If you're far enough away from retirement and hate your job so much that you simply can't stand the thought of sticking it out until retirement age, at least find out what you'd be giving up if you left. Then use that information in your negotiations with your new employer. ("See what I'm giving up to come work for you?")

Since your pension is based on salary and years of service, the other two things you may be able to do to increase your pension are earn more money and/or stay longer at the company. Starting now, get to know your pension plan inside and out. Read the summary plan description and talk to your benefits administrator about your expected benefits and what you can do to preserve or increase them. Understand that as you get closer to retirement, your pension becomes an increasingly valuable asset. Take care of it.

COLLECTING YOUR PENSION: LUMP SUM OR ANNUITY?

Now back to the two big decisions you'll be faced with when you retire. The first decision is whether you want to take your pension all at once in a lump sum or in dribs and drabs in the form of an annuity. When you retire, your company probably will ask which you prefer. They'll tell you what your monthly check will be if you choose the annuity and what the lump sum will be if you take your pension all at once. Before your eyes pop out of your head at the biggest dollar amount you've ever seen with your name on it, understand that the lump sum is simply the present value of all the annuity payments you would have received if you had elected that option. Using actuarial tables and the time value of money, the company estimates your life expectancy and applies the appropriate interest rate to translate the stream of future annuity payments into a lump sum handed to you today. Theoretically, from a dollars-and-cents point of view, the two options are equal.

But when you look at your own financial situation and see how the two options play out in retirement, they are far from equal.

Why Taking a Lump-Sum Distribution Is Preferable to an Annuity

Your company may need to be impartial when telling you about your retirement options, but we don't have to be. We work with lots of retirees, talk to other financial professionals who work with lots of retirees, and have direct experience with how the numbers work out in real life. We're convinced it's better to take a lump sum instead of an annuity. Here's why.

You Control the Asset

When you take your pension distribution as a lump sum, it becomes yours to do with as you please. Now, you could probably go out and buy a French villa and have enough left over for a Maserati, but we don't mean that kind of control. The kind of control we're talking about is the power to invest it in a manner that would net you more income over your lifetime than the annuity would have provided. It may help to pause here and talk a little bit about how annuities work: If you chose the annuity, your company would take the pension money due you and buy an annuity policy from an insurance company. (If you work for a large company, it may handle the payouts without going to an outside insurance company, but the concept is the same.) The insurance company would take your money and invest it. However, no matter how smart the insurance company is in investing your money (the money really isn't yours anymore, once it's turned over to the insurance company), you would never receive more than the monthly payments the insurance company promised you when you signed up. Now, some people are perfectly happy with this arrangement. They like the fact that the insurance company assumes all the investment and life expectancy risks while the retiree is assured of receiving a fixed amount of money every month for life. But this transfer of risk can be costly. The interest rate assumption used to calculate the monthly payments is usually quite low, somewhere around the rate on U.S. Treasury bills. Meanwhile, the insurance company is pocketing the spread between what it earns on your used-to-be pension money and what it is obligated to pay you every month. By dialing up your risk tolerance just a notch, you can take the lump sum, invest it in a diversified portfolio of securities, and basically do what the insurance company is doing. Why should they get rich at your expense? Besides, you're going to need the extra money when your postretirement expenses start going up. Which brings us to reason number 2 for taking the lump sum . . .

You Have a Better Chance of Keeping Up with Inflation

If you take the annuity, and if it does not have cost-of-living adjustments (COLAs) built in—most don't—your odds of keeping up with inflation are zero. Your first monthly check will be the same as your last, even though there may be a span of twenty or thirty years between the two. In that time your expenses could double or even triple. If you have a hard time imagining a future with $8 loaves of bread and $50,000 Honda Accords, think back twenty or thirty years. What was your grocery bill in 1970? What was your income back then? Could you live on that amount now? It can be tempting to take the bird in the hand when you're offered seemingly risk-free annuity payments, but as too many retirees found out during the inflationary 1970s and 1980s, those fixed monthly payments entail another form of risk: purchasing power risk. Income that fails to keep up with expenses will not be of much use to you in your later years. And if you should have an emergency and need to get your hands on additional funds, too bad. So take the lump sum, invest it wisely, draw income from it in a sensible manner, and it should last you a lifetime, if not longer—which brings us to reason number 3 for taking the lump sum . . .

You Can Avoid Disinheriting Your Children

Annuities usually keep paying as long as the retiree is alive (or as long as the surviving spouse is alive, if it's a joint-and-survivor annuity). When the last person dies, the checks stop coming. It doesn't matter how much pension money you turned over to the insurance company at the time of your retirement, and it doesn't matter how many payments you received before kicking the bucket. When you're dead, the money is gone. If you take the lump sum, on the other hand, invest it wisely, and draw income sensibly, whatever is left at the time of your death goes to your heirs. If you can't make up your own mind between the lump sum or the annuity, ask your children. They'll tell you which choice they think you should make.

And Another Thing

The most important thing to remember about the annuity is that once you've chosen it, you can't go back and change your mind. Once you elect to receive a check for life, you give up all rights to any lump sum that may have once been offered you. On the other hand, if you take the lump sum and decide later on that you really would like to have a guaranteed income, you can always go out and buy an annuity from the insurance company of your choice. By the way, the kind of annuity we're talking about as a pension option is different from the kind of annuity you may be familiar with as an investment vehicle. We love annuities as investment vehicles. They provide tax-deferred compounding and have certain protection features that make them good investments for older people who want to see their money grow without taking on a lot of risk. But you can invest in an annuity for growth without converting it to an income stream. This is called *annuitizing*, and we have a real problem with that because it requires you to give up all your money in exchange for the promise of lifetime income. You're much better off controlling the money yourself, taking withdrawals as you need them and leaving the rest to grow.

WHAT TO DO ABOUT TAXES

As you might have guessed, Uncle Sam will have his hand out if you decide to take receipt of this very large sum of money. But he does offer a special way to pay the taxes, which we'll get to in a minute. By the way, if you elect to receive your pension in the form of an annuity, each check you receive will probably be fully taxable as ordinary income. Keep in mind that pensions consist largely of money that has never been taxed; any after-tax contributions you might have made to the plan would not be taxed again, but the bulk, if not all, of your pension consists of pretax contributions made by you and/or your employer, plus the earnings on those contributions. These pretax contributions and earnings will someday have to be taxed, but the longer you can put off that unfortunate event, the better. Once again, the annuity gives you less control by forcing you to pay taxes whether you want to or not.

Now, when it comes to explaining the various tax rules about lump sum distributions (including 401[k] plan distributions), we could put you to sleep by quoting parts of the tax code and being completely impartial in our explanations of the tax alternatives. You'll be happy to know we're not going to do that. Instead, we're going to reveal our biases up front and tell you—based on our real-world experiences—what we've found works. At the same time we take this stand, we also acknowledge that your situation could be different and that the recommendations being dispensed here could be all wrong for you. So be sure to apply this information to your own circumstances, get professional help if you need it, and make up your own mind.

The easiest way to put off paying taxes on your lump-sum distribution is not to ever get your hands on it, but rather let it pass right over your head into an IRA rollover account. Sorry you'll miss out on the experience of seeing such a huge check made out in your name, but believe us, you wouldn't want to pay for that experience. If you take receipt of the money, 20% will be missing right off the bat for tax withholding. Then when you file your tax return, the IRS will want some explanation of how you intend to pay the rest of the tax, if the 20 percent didn't cover it. Now, the IRS isn't a complete mercenary when it comes to taxing lump-sum distributions. Because these distributions are so unusual, the IRS offers a special tax formula, called forward averaging, which lets you pay the tax as if the distribution had been spread over a period of five or ten years. (Forward averaging is being phased out and may be gone by the time you read this). We're not going to get into the specifics of forward averaging except to say that it is a favorable tax rate and you pay it only once, not over a period of five or ten years as the name would imply. The reason you might want to take receipt of your lump-sum distribution and pay the tax up front is because the tax rate is quite favorable compared to ordinary income tax rates. However, it's still a lot of money, and most people are better off keeping it away from Uncle Sam as long as possible and investing it. The longer that money stays in a tax-sheltered account to compound, the more you will likely have at the end, even if you eventually have to pay taxes on it at a higher rate.

Which brings us to another point. If you take receipt of your lump-sum distribution and pay the taxes on it up front, what are you going to do with what's left? Assuming you'll pass on the French villa and Maserati and instead put it into an investment account to grow, you'll be faced with yearly tax consequences on your investment returns. So let's say you invest $500,000 in mutual funds that grow an average of 12 percent the first year. That's $60,000 of taxable income you'll have to report in year 1. If you're in the 15 percent tax bracket, that's $9,000 in taxes. If the $500,000 were instead invested in a tax-sheltered IRA rollover account, you wouldn't have to report the $60,000 in investment earnings, and the $9,000 (or more) that you would otherwise have to take out for taxes can stay in the account to grow. With the IRA rollover account, you report income—and pay taxes on it—as you receive it. That gives you much more control over when and how to pay the taxes. (Until you reach age 70½, when there are some rules you have to follow; we'll get to those in Chapter 9.)

Obviously, we're convinced it's better to defer taxes by putting a lump-sum distribution into an IRA rollover account, but if you want to be sure that's the right course of action for you, ask your accountant or financial planner to run the numbers. The calculation will need to take into account your current and expected tax rates and make some assumptions about your income needs and life expectancy.

WHAT IF YOU HAVE NO CHOICE?

What if your company doesn't offer your pension in a lump sum but rather insists that you take it in monthly payments? Well, you'll accept it graciously and find other ways to keep up with inflation. If you're lucky enough to have a 401(k) in addition to the pension, you can roll that over to an IRA account and let it build up so you'll be able to draw from it when your pension income is no longer enough. If you do not have a 401(k) or any other assets that you can let grow for the future, you may have to scale back your lifestyle and try to put part of your monthly pension check into savings. You may even want to work for a few years so you can stash money away for the future. The most important thing to remember when you're settling into retirement is that even if everything looks good on paper now—your income appears to be sufficient to meet your needs—that situation is unlikely to last. You've got to have a cushion.

CHAPTER NINE

Individual Retirement Accounts

A little and a little collected together become a great deal;
the heap in the barn consists of single grains,
and drop by drop make the inundation.

—Sa'di

In Chapter 6, we talked generally about how to invest your retirement savings, including any individual retirement accounts (IRAs) you have. Here we go into the mechanics of how these accounts work.

HOW TO CHOOSE A CUSTODIAN FOR YOUR IRA ROLLOVER ACCOUNT

If you've never had an IRA before, you may feel some trepidation about putting the biggest lump sum you've ever seen into an account that has rules about how and when you can get at your money. The reason you won't be laying eyes on the lump sum is that you will have your company send it directly to your IRA custodian in order to avoid the 20 percent withholding tax, remember? This means you'll need to get the account set up in advance so you can tell your company where to send the check.

An IRA custodian is an institution that has been authorized by the Internal Revenue Service to hold IRA assets. The reason you can't keep your IRA money under your mattress at home is that then the IRS couldn't keep tabs on it. And since IRAs consist of money that has never been taxed, the IRS wants to keep a close watch on funds flowing in and out of the account so it can assess the appropriate taxes (and penalties, if applicable). IRA custodians are required to report this kind of activity, even if you'd just as soon keep it a secret. If it seems like there are a lot of rules connected with IRAs, you're right. (Wait till you read the sections that follow.) But it's well worth learning these rules and following them; the amount of extra money you'll get to keep as a result of deferring taxes on your invested lump sum is pretty amazing. If you don't believe it, ask your accountant or financial planner to run the numbers for you.

So before you say good-bye to your company, go out and find a trusted institution to serve as your IRA custodian. By the way, if you've been investing personal funds for years, you may already have relationships established with brokerage firms or mutual funds. If you feel comfortable continuing with these relationships, and if you feel your present advisors are qualified to handle the complexities of retirement distributions and the other financial issues you face at this time, go ahead and continue with those relationships. But now that your finances have suddenly become more complicated, this may be a good time to reevaluate all of your financial relationships and consider shopping around for advisors who specialize in serving retirees.

When choosing an IRA custodian, you first need to think about how you will invest the assets. Some custodians, like banks, offer limited investment choices. Mutual funds are also restrictive because you have to stay within that family of funds. For the most flexibility—and remember, you'll be keeping this account for a long time—open a self-directed IRA account at a brokerage firm. With this type of account you can buy individual stocks and bonds and also choose from among thousands of mutual funds. And you can move your money around all you want, most likely starting out in the money market fund until you decide what to do and then moving into specific investments according to your investment plan. (See Chapter 6.) Later on, if you decide those initial investments aren't right for you, you can sell them and buy something else. The whole time you are moving the money around, it is staying under the tax-sheltered IRA umbrella and the IRS has no idea what you're doing. Nor does it care. It's only when you pull money out of the account that IRS ears perk up.

HOW TO TAKE MONEY OUT OF AN IRA

It is very easy to get money out of an IRA. All you have to do is call the custodian and tell it to issue you a check. Of course, you must have liquid funds in the account, or else you'll have to sell enough stock or mutual fund shares to cover the amount you need. Getting your hands on the money is never a problem with an IRA. If you ask the custodian to send you a check, it has to do it. (There may be a waiting period of a few days, if investments have to be liquidated.) It's the tax (and possibly penalty) consequences of that little transaction that you need to be concerned about. After the custodian issues you a check, it will report the disbursement to the IRS. The IRS will then be watching for it on your tax return.

IF YOU ARE UNDER AGE 59½

The rules say that if you are under 59½ and take money out of a regular IRA account (we're not dealing with nondeductible IRAs or the new Roth IRA here because lump-sum distributions go into regular IRA accounts), you must pay a federal penalty tax of 10 percent of the amount of the withdrawal, plus ordinary income tax. The reason for this is that IRAs are designed to be *retirement* accounts. Since the IRS is giving up a lot by letting you defer taxes on your investment earnings, there must be some kind of disincentive against people using their IRAs as regular investment accounts that they can tap at will for things like vacations and new cars. But when you think about it, 10 percent isn't that big a penalty if you really need the money. While we certainly do not recommend tapping your IRA if you're under age 59½ (mainly because you're going to need the money later), it may be comforting to know that you can get at it if you need to, and all it will cost you is 10 percent plus ordinary income tax (which you'd have to pay someday anyway).

There are a few ways around this 10 percent penalty, however. One is designed for people who are retiring early and will be making regular withdrawals from their IRA account (whether that's the case or not). If you set up a schedule of *substantially equal periodic payments* designed to exhaust your IRA over your life expectancy, and if you continue with these payments for at least five years or until you reach age 59½ (whichever occurs later), you will not have to pay the 10 percent penalty. If you decide to do this, get professional help because the amount must be calculated properly.

Other exceptions to the 10 percent penalty have to do with how the money is used. If you use it to buy a first house for yourself, your kids, your grandkids, or your parents, you can take out up to $10,000 without paying the 10 percent penalty. If you use it for higher education expenses for yourself, your spouse, your kids, or your grandkids, you can take out whatever it costs for tuition, fees, books, supplies, and equipment and not pay the 10 percent penalty. If you get hit with large medical expenses in a year, you can take out enough to offset the deductible portion of the expenses without paying the 10 percent penalty. And if you lose your job, you can take out enough to pay health insurance premiums for yourself and your family.

The other two ways of getting around the 10 percent penalty are not recommended: If you become disabled or die, you (or your heirs) can have unlimited access to your IRA without penalty (but not taxes).

IF YOU ARE BETWEEN AGES 59½ AND 70½

If you are between the ages of 59½ and 70½, there are no restrictions on taking money out of your IRA. You can take any amount you want, any time you want. Just make sure you report the income on your tax return, or the IRS will come looking for you.

IF YOU ARE AGE 70½ OR OLDER

You know that nice tax deferral you've been getting all these years? The one that's allowed your retirement distribution to grow to heretofore unimagined sums? Well, the IRS says enough's enough. When you reach age 70½, you have to start paying taxes by withdrawing a specified minimum amount from your IRA each year and declaring that income on your tax return. It doesn't matter if you've been withdrawing money all along. Everybody who turns 70½ has to take the minimum required distribution according to a certain formula, regardless of how much they've already withdrawn and regardless of whether they need the money or not.

The penalty for not taking the minimum mandatory distribution is 50 percent of the amount that should have been withdrawn. Note that this is no measly amount like the 10 percent early withdrawal penalty. This 50 percent excise tax is one of the stiffest penalties in the tax code, so we urge you not to mess with it. If you are nearing age 70½, learn these rules and comply with them. The fact that they're rather complicated is no excuse. Either get out your calculator and life expectancy tables or be prepared to pay your accountant to do it for you. In any case, make sure you withdraw the required amount and report it to the IRS. Please note that it is not your custodian's responsibility to tell you how much you should withdraw. Some custodians may do this as a courtesy, but there are three good reasons why you need to take responsibility for this yourself: First, the custodian isn't the one who will pay the penalty if there's an error in the calculation; you will. Second, if you've been contributing to IRAs all along, or have divided your IRA into several accounts for estate planning purposes, theoretically you could have many different IRA accounts all over town. No one custodian would know the total value of all your accounts or be able to calculate the exact amount you need to withdraw. Third, there are some decisions you need to make about how you want the minimum required distribution calculated; you want to understand your options and make an informed decision rather than leaving it up to the custodian.

That said, here's fair warning that the following material is technical, dry, and boring, if you (1) are nowhere near age 70½ and couldn't be bothered learning rules you have no use for yet or (2) are over 70½, have been taking minimum mandatory withdrawals for years, and probably know the rules better than we do. If either of these applies, please feel free to skip ahead to more interesting material, like beneficiary designations.

Before getting into the specifics of minimum mandatory distributions, it's important to understand that these are indeed *minimums*. Once you turn 59½, you can take any amount out of your IRA anytime you want. Turning 70½ simply means you *must* take a required minimum amount each year; you can always take more than that if you wish.

When the First Withdrawal Must Be Made

On January 1 of the year you turn 70½, you need to start thinking about taking your first minimum mandatory distribution. You actually have until April 1 of the following year, or fifteen whole months, before you have to take the money out of the account, but you should start thinking about it early. For one thing, the distribution will be based on the value of the account as of the December 31 that just passed. When you get your year-end IRA account statement sometime during the month of January, you'll want to keep it in a safe place so you can refer to it when the time comes to calculate your minimum mandatory withdrawal. The second thing is that although you have until April 1 of the following year to take your first minimum mandatory distribution, you'll want to take it before December 31. If you wait until April 1 of the following year, you'll end up taking two taxable distributions in one year, because the first year is the only year you get a grace period to April 1. After that, you have to take your minimum withdrawal by December 31.

Calculating the Minimum Mandatory Distribution

How do you know how much to take out? Well, the first thing you do is add up the value of all your IRA accounts as of December 31 of the year before you turn 70½. Next, you divide that number by either your life expectancy or the combined life expectancy of you and your beneficiary, as indicated in the IRS life expectancy tables. According to the tables, a 70-year-old person has a life expectancy of 16 years. If his or her spouse is also 70, their combined life expectancy is 20.6 years. So if your IRAs were worth, say, $300,000 on December 31, 1999, you'd have to take out $18,750 by December 31, 2000, if you used your own life expectancy ($300,000 ÷ 16 = $18,750), or $14,563 if you used the joint life expectancy of you and your same-age beneficiary ($300,000 ÷ 20.6 = $14,563). Your numbers will be different, of course, depending on the value of your IRAs and the age of your beneficiary.

As this example shows, if you are interested in taking the least amount in order to save the most taxes (remember, you can always take out more than the minimum), you'll want to use the combined life expectancy of you and your beneficiary. Most people name their spouse as beneficiary (for reasons we'll go into later), but you can name anybody you want. If the person you name as beneficiary is 10 or more years younger than you (say it's a child or grandchild), you have to assume, for minimum withdrawal purposes, that the beneficiary is exactly ten years younger.

In addition to deciding whose life expectancy(ies) you want to use, you also have to decide how the calculations will be performed in subsequent years. The easy way is to reduce the life expectancy by one year each time you make your annual withdrawal. This is called the *term certain* method. So if, for simplicity's sake, you were basing your withdrawals on your own life expectancy (rather than the joint life expectancy of you and your beneficiary), and your first year's life expectancy was 16 years, the next year it would be 15 years, then 14, and so on. The problem with this method is that, by age 86, the money is gone, even if you're not dead yet.

A possibly better way is to recalculate your life expectancy every year. This is called the *recalculation* method and assumes that the longer you live, the longer you're expected to live. Although it's more complicated, it reduces the risk that you will outlive your money and lets you take out a smaller amount each year than the term certain method. However, if you choose the recalculation method and your beneficiary dies before you do, your beneficiary's life expectancy becomes zero and you have to switch from joint to single life expectancy, which will accelerate the withdrawals. Then when you die, the entire IRA balance must be distributed in one year. Although the term certain method just described runs the risk of exhausting the IRA while you and/or your beneficiary are still alive, the advantage it holds over the recalculation method is that you don't have to worry about unexpectedly having to accelerate (and pay taxes on) the withdrawals, and your heirs would not be hit with a big taxable inheritance in one year.

Some people attempt to get around these drawbacks by using the *hybrid* method. This is where you would use term certain for your own life expectancy and recalculation for your spouse's life expectancy (or vice versa). Some financial planners believe this helps equalize the lack of gender bias in the IRS life expectancy tables, since in the tables men are presumed to live as long as women even though real-life statistics do not bear this out. Since the hybrid method offers several combinations, each with different tax consequences depending on your age, your beneficiary's age, and how long you and your beneficiary can reasonably be expected to live, you should talk to a professional about your options if you are seriously interested in saving taxes for your heirs. At the very least, get a copy of IRS Publication 590, which contains all the specifics and tables needed to make the calculations. It is available without charge and can be obtained by calling 800-TAX-FORM or visiting www.irs.gov on the Internet.

While we're on the subject of life expectancy, we need to take this opportunity to remind you to use the IRS tables for the purpose of calculating minimum IRA withdrawals only. Do not assume that just because the IRS says you'll live to age 86 you should plan to have all your money run out at that time. What if you live to age 90 or 95? What will you live on then? The IRS doesn't care; it already got its tax money. From a statistical point of view, life expectancy means that, based on previous mortality experiences, half of all 70-year-olds can be expected to live longer than sixteen years and half can be expected to die before then. You are not a statistic. You are a real person. If you want to make sure you do not outlive your money, you need to estimate your own life expectancy with greater accuracy based on your health and genetic makeup. Follow the IRS rules for minimum mandatory distributions, but make sure the rest of your financial plan is designed to carry you well into your 90s.

Making the Withdrawal

If you have more than one IRA, the IRS doesn't care from which account you take your minimum mandatory withdrawal. You can take it all from one account or spread it over several accounts. The important thing is to complete the withdrawal sometime during the calendar year.

WHAT HAPPENS TO YOUR IRA AFTER YOU DIE?

At the time you sign up for your IRA, you will be asked to make a beneficiary designation. If you're not sure what that means, you'll be told that your beneficiary is the person who will get your IRA assets when you die. So you jot down the name of your spouse or your kid(s) and put the matter out of your mind. After all, you have no intention of dying anytime soon. But your beneficiary designation is a very important decision. Not only do you want to make sure your assets pass to the right person, you also want to minimize taxes for your loved ones. And as noted earlier, your beneficiary designation will also determine your minimum mandatory withdrawal schedule and therefore your tax liability from age 70½ on.

IF YOUR BENEFICIARY IS YOUR SPOUSE

The IRA succession rules are very supportive of marriage vows. When you name your spouse as beneficiary, after your death your IRA assets can pass to him or her with minimal—if any—

tax consequences. Your spouse can avoid current taxation by rolling over your IRA into his or her own account, just as you did with your lump-sum distribution from your pension. Your spouse would then treat the IRA as his or her own, naming a new beneficiary, and even combining assets with any previous IRAs he or she may have. The investments would continue to grow tax-deferred, and income would be reported for tax purposes only as it is withdrawn. The under-59½ early withdrawal penalties and over-70½ minimum distribution requirements would apply as usual based on your spouse's age. The other tax benefit relates to estate taxes: Any assets going to your spouse would qualify for the unlimited marital deduction and therefore would not be subject to estate taxes at the time of your death.

IF YOUR BENEFICIARY IS SOMEONE OTHER THAN YOUR SPOUSE

If you name a child, grandchild, friend, same-sex partner, or anyone other than a spouse as your beneficiary, he or she or they may not roll the assets into their own IRA. Instead, they have to follow certain rules about when to receive (and pay taxes on) the assets. If you are over 70½ at the time of your death, your beneficiary(ies) must continue taking withdrawals at least as fast as your minimum mandatory distribution schedule would have required. (They can always take more, but each withdrawal will be taxable, of course.) If you are under 70½ at the time of your death, your beneficiary must start taking withdrawals within a year and must schedule the withdrawals according to his or her life expectancy. It is for this reason that people sometimes name children or grandchildren as their beneficiary: The younger the beneficiary is, the longer the taxable withdrawals can be spread out.

IF YOUR BENEFICIARY IS A TRUST

People who have a lot of estate planning issues to think about— say they want to be able to direct the disposition of the assets after a spouse's death or the person they want to leave the assets to is not competent to manage them—sometimes name a trust as their IRA beneficiary. Trusts are very complicated, and if you have one (or are thinking about getting one), your estate planning attorney will guide you.

IF YOUR BENEFICIARY IS A CHARITY

You can direct your IRA assets to go to a private foundation or charity. In this case, your minimum mandatory distribution schedule would be based on your single life expectancy, and at your death the assets would go to the charity, bypassing your estate.

IF YOU FAIL TO NAME A BENEFICIARY

If you die without having named a beneficiary, your IRA will be part of your estate. In this case, the assets will be taxed sooner than with the other options. If you have not yet started taking minimum mandatory distributions at the time of your death, the IRA must be emptied within five years by the beneficiary(ies) of your estate. If you have already begun taking minimum mandatory distributions and were using the term certain method, the IRA must be drained according to the original schedule. If you've been taking minimum mandatory distributions using the recalculation method, the IRA must be exhausted within a year. The exception to these rather stiff distribution requirements is when your spouse is the sole beneficiary of your estate, he or she can roll the IRA over into his or her own account as described earlier, even if his or her name is not listed on the IRA beneficiary form.

IF YOU NAME THE WRONG BENEFICIARY

What if you get divorced and remarry without changing your beneficiary? Will your ex-spouse get your IRA? What if you want your assets equally divided among your three grandchildren and a fourth one comes along? Will that innocent child be excluded from your bequest? We don't want to speculate how difficult it might be to have your real wishes carried out from beyond the grave, so we'll just say this: Stay on top of your beneficiary designation while you're still around to do so. Change it as appropriate whenever there's a birth, death, divorce, or marriage, and incorporate it with any other estate planning strategies that you may be using. Also, make sure your IRA custodian agrees to carry out your wishes. Many custodians are not very sophisticated when it comes to estate planning strategies or minimum mandatory distribution calculations, and the forms are often too limited to state exactly what you want. Above all, don't treat this subject lightly. The last thing you want after a lifetime of toil is for a big chunk of your wealth to go to the wrong person or to the federal government in taxes.

SHOULD YOU CONTRIBUTE TO AN IRA AFTER YOU'VE RETIRED?

Our discussion so far has dealt with rollover IRAs because that's where the bulk of your assets will be after you receive the proceeds from your corporate pension plan(s). But you may also want to contribute $2,000 a year to an IRA, as long as you have at least that much in earned income. Even though you may be drawing income from your rollover IRA account, you may still want to contribute to either a regular IRA or a Roth IRA. The choice will depend on whether you think your tax bracket will rise or fall between now and the time you take the money out and how long you think you'll live.

CONTRIBUTE TO A REGULAR IRA IF YOU THINK YOUR TAX BRACKET WILL GO DOWN

If you are under age 70½ and in a high tax bracket, because you are still working or have other sources of taxable income, you can contribute $2,000 to a regular IRA and knock about $560 off your current tax bill, if you are in the 28 percent tax bracket. If you're married and have at least $4,000 in earned income between the two of you, you can contribute $4,000 ($2,000 to each IRA) and save $1,120 in taxes. It probably makes sense to do this if you will be in a lower tax bracket later on when you take the money out. Still, take a look at the Roth IRA, described next, because it offers additional benefits above and beyond the regular IRA.

CONTRIBUTE TO A ROTH IRA IF YOU THINK YOUR TAX BRACKET WILL GO UP OR STAY THE SAME (OR IF YOU PLAN TO LIVE A LONG TIME)

If you think your tax bracket will stay the same or go up, you can contribute to a Roth IRA, forgo the current tax deduction, and take tax-free withdrawals later on. As with a regular IRA, your investments will grow tax-deferred. But you never have to pay taxes on the money as it comes out, as long as it's been in there at least five years or you have attained age 59½. (Your contributions can be taken out tax-free at any time.) Perhaps the best part about a Roth IRA for retired people is that you don't have to take minimum mandatory withdrawals at age 70½. You can also keep contributing past the age of 70½ (as long as you have earned income). It is this feature that makes the Roth IRA such a good planning vehicle: With your regular and/or rollover IRAs designed to exhaust according to your life expectancy (as defined by the IRS), your Roth IRA can be an ace in the hole in case you stay on this planet a long time. If you are 70 now, and contribute $2,000 to a Roth IRA for ten years, you'll have nearly $30,000 at age 80, assuming a modest 8 percent return. Just remember that you must have at least $2,000 in earned income in order to contribute the full $2,000, and your adjusted gross income can be no higher than $110,000 if you're single or $160,000 if you and your spouse file a joint return.

CHAPTER TEN

Real Estate

Real estate is the closest thing to the
proverbial pot of gold.

—Ada Louise Huxtable

ou know what they say about land: They ain't making any
more of it. That doesn't mean it's always a good investment,
of course. There's plenty of land in the desert or in locations far
from cities and towns that people aren't much interested in buying. Still, it's the scarcity factor that gives real estate its appeal as
an investment and makes it an excellent hedge against inflation.
Although real estate is generally considered a nonliquid investment—better to buy and hold for its potential appreciation over
a long period of time—there are ways to generate income from
real estate. One is by tapping the equity in your home. The other
is by investing in income property or a special type of security
called a real estate investment trust (REIT).

TAPPING THE EQUITY IN YOUR HOME

If you've owned your home for many years and have not been
tapping the equity for things like college, weddings, or credit

card debt, you may be sitting on a gold mine. There are several ways to convert home equity into retirement income. You may want to take advantage of them early in your retirement or save them until later, after you've used up other resources first.

When you read this chapter, also keep family members in mind. If you have aging parents who are sitting on a ton of equity but have little current income, why preserve your inheritance when your parents need the money now? You can help them by looking into one of the home equity conversion strategies to be discussed, perhaps even keeping the financing within the family to save fees and get tax benefits for yourself. If you do decide to enter into a loan arrangement with your parents, make sure you comply with all the tax laws. The IRS doesn't like monkey business going on between family members when it's done purely to avoid taxes.

Following are some ways to unlock the equity in your home.

SELL YOUR HOUSE AND BUY A CHEAPER ONE

With the kids out of the nest, no job to keep you tied to your present location, and no time to maintain a big house what with all the traveling you intend to do, you may decide to sell your big house and move to a smaller one. If so, you can take advantage of one of the biggest windfalls of the Taxpayer Relief Act of 1997 and its subsequent "technical correction" in May 1998 to sell your house and pay virtually no capital gains taxes. The law allows single taxpayers to exclude up to $250,000 and married couples up to $500,000 in gains, as long as they've lived in the house for two out of five years before the sale. The previous rules about being age 55 or rolling over the equity to another home are gone. And for what it's worth, you can do this several times during your lifetime. Selling your big house and buying a smaller one accomplishes two goals: It releases some equity, which you can put into your retirement bucket and draw income as you need it. It also simplifies your lifestyle by giving you less house to maintain.

SELL YOUR HOUSE AND RENT

Now that the law does not require you to buy another house within a certain time period in order to get the capital gains tax break, you may want to rent for a while—maybe even indefinitely. If you've been a slave to your house for many years, you'll appreciate the freedom renting can give you. You don't have to worry about repairs, because the landlord does them for you. You can move anytime you want without worrying about selling your house and getting enough out of it to cover the real estate and escrow fees. And perhaps the best part is that you'll have a whole pile of money in the bank because you won't be plunking it into another home. You can put the proceeds from the sale of your house into your retirement bucket, invest it along with whatever else is in the bucket, and draw enough income to pay rent and other expenses. For example, let's say you net $200,000 from the sale of your house. If you invest it at 10 percent, you'll earn $20,000 a year. If you draw 8 percent income (allowing the other 2 percent to grow), that's $16,000 a year, or $1,333 a month—enough to cover rent in most places.

If you're worried about losing the ongoing tax break that home ownership provides through the deductibility of mortgage interest, you may want to take a fresh look at your tax situation. For one thing, your tax bracket may be lower in retirement. For another, when you factor in maintenance, repairs, property taxes, and insurance, home ownership may not put you ahead after all. If you're a numbers person, you or your accountant can do some calculations to see what would be best for you. But since the numbers are often very close, a better way to approach the rent-vs.-buy decision may be to look at your goals and overall lifestyle. If freedom, mobility, and simplicity are important to you, think about renting. If stability and pride of ownership are values you cherish, think about buying.

STAY WHERE YOU ARE

If you love your home and can't bear the thought of moving, there are several ways you can free up some of your equity for retirement income without giving up your beloved abode.

Reverse Mortgage

Reverse mortgages are designed to allow retirees to stay in their homes and enjoy the use of the equity now, when they need it, rather than passing it on to heirs after they're gone. With a reverse mortgage you borrow against the equity in your home. But unlike a regular home loan, you don't have to make monthly payments or worry about paying off the mortgage. Instead, the lender pays you. Generally, the payments continue for the rest of your life or until you move. Then when you die or sell your house, you or your heirs pay back the loan plus interest, and keep any proceeds that remain. In no case will you have to cough up additional funds to pay off the loan. That's the beauty of reverse mortgages: The lender takes the risk that you will live a long time or that the house may not appreciate at the expected rate. You pay for this transfer of risk, of course, which is why you'll want to think carefully about this strategy and shop around for the best deal.

To qualify, you must be at least 62 and live in your home. The amount you get depends on your age, how much your house is worth, and current interest rates. The greatest cash amounts generally go to the oldest borrowers living in the homes of greatest value on loans with the lowest costs. Generally, you can expect to receive 30 to 75 percent of your property value, but some of the proceeds will have to be used to pay off any existing mortgages. The payments are not taxable and don't affect Social Security benefits. Interest costs can be deducted when the house is sold.

When shopping, be sure to explore all of your options so you can decide which plan is best for you. And be sure to compare the costs and benefits offered by competing lenders. Some reverse mortgages let you take a lump sum all at once (great fodder for your retirement bucket!); others offer a line of credit so you can write a check whenever you need it. Some offer competitive interest rates and fees; others take advantage of the obscure nature of these instruments to gouge unsuspecting homeowners, in some cases even cutting themselves in on part of the future appreciation of the home. Some offer high credit limits; others, such as those offered through Fannie Mae (FNMA) have lower limits but may offer more attractive terms. Be sure to get counseling before signing onto one of these deals. Talk with loan counselors who understand the intricacies of these arrangements as well as your own advisors who understand your financial situation and will be watching out for your best interests.

The American Association of Retired Persons (AARP) has a wealth of information on reverse mortgages, including a forty-seven-page booklet called "Homemade Money." To receive a free copy, send a self-addressed postcard to AARP Home Equity Information Center, 601 E Street NW, Washington, D.C. 20049.

Borrowing Against Your Children's Inheritance

When you take out a reverse mortgage, you are essentially borrowing against your children's inheritance, so why not keep the financing within the family? You'd need a lawyer to set this up, but if you take out a reverse mortgage with one of your children, your offspring would pay you a fixed sum equal to a certain percentage of the equity in your home. You get the cash, your child gets certain tax benefits, and you'll all save high lender's fees.

Sale Leaseback

With a sale leaseback you sell your house to an investor (maybe one of your kids?), who immediately rents it back to you on a long-term (often lifetime) lease. Unlike a reverse mortgage in which you retain the title to the house, a sale leaseback is an outright sale. You receive a down payment plus regular monthly payments. Sale leaseback contracts can be written a variety of ways, but generally the new owner takes over expenses such as taxes, repairs, and insurance. These transactions are complicated and have significant tax implications, so be sure to consult a professional advisor, even if (*especially* if) you are keeping the deal within the family.

Rent Out Part of Your House

Not all methods for obtaining income from your home have to involve complicated rules and fine print. You could simply rent out a room or two to a student or couple—maybe to another retiree who decided to sell her house and rent—and receive several hundred dollars a month in rent. You'll want to be careful when selecting your tenant, of course, since you'll be living under the same roof. Before placing an ad in the paper or posting a notice on a public bulletin board, ask among your circle of friends and acquaintances if anyone is looking for a place to live. By choosing someone you're compatible with, you may get the additional bonus of companionship, which can be nice if you live alone. With a tenant or "roommate," you can both watch out for each other at the same time you're providing economic benefit to one another.

REAL ESTATE AS AN INVESTMENT

Once you've decided what to do about your primary residence, you may want to expand your investment in real estate to take advantage of its appreciation potential, tax benefits, and even current income. As noted earlier, real estate provides a good hedge against inflation, since real estate prices tend to rise when inflation is rising. So if your asset allocation plan from Chapter 6 calls for all of your assets to be divided among stocks, bonds, and cash, you may also want to consider allocating a portion—say 5 to 10 percent—to real estate in case inflation rears its ugly head again, as it did in the late 1970s. Even without the threat of inflation, real estate can be a good long-term investment, primarily because it allows you to use leverage to get a bigger bang for your buck. For example, if you buy a $200,000 property and put $20,000 down, and if the property appreciates 10 percent to $220,000, you have just doubled your investment. There are drawbacks to real estate, of course—leverage being one of them. You could lose your entire investment and more if the property declines in value. However, if you're careful and know what you're doing, real estate may have a place in your overall investment portfolio.

OWNERSHIP OF INCOME PROPERTY

You know those repairs we said your landlord would make if you decide to sell your house and rent? Well, you'll get to do those repairs for someone else if you decide to become a landlord and invest part of your savings in income property such as apartments, duplexes, condos, or a single-family residence that you rent out to somebody else. Why in the world would you want to do that? Because rent can be good income. And depending on the location of the property and what the rental market looks like, it can be a source of constantly rising income. If rents are going up by, say, 3 to 5 percent a year, you have a built-in inflation hedge to cover higher expenses in retirement. And the whole time you're collecting rent from your tenants, you're holding onto a property that has a good chance of increasing in value. Not only that, but there are tax benefits to being a landlord.

However, there are substantial drawbacks to owning income property too, and those repairs we just talked about are not the worst of it. You have to find the right tenants and hope they don't trash the place. The property could sit vacant for a month or two (or more) while you fix it up or find new tenants; meanwhile you're missing out on the rental income for those months. The property may not rise in value as much as you had hoped, so that after paying all of the expenses (mortgage interest, insurance, property taxes, etc.), you could end up breaking even or losing money.

But you decide. Some former landlords swear they'll never do it again. Others find the business of renting property highly lucrative and even fun. Just be sure you know what you're getting into. Take the time to understand the real estate laws in your state, become familiar with the real estate rental market in your area, and be prepared to devote considerable time and attention to the endeavor. Unlike stocks, where somebody else is running the company you are investing in, real estate is a high-maintenance investment—and we mean that quite literally.

REAL ESTATE INVESTMENT TRUSTS (REITs)

One way you can avoid getting calls in the middle of the night about broken water pipes is to invest in income property through a real estate investment trust, or REIT. A REIT works like a mutual fund, where investors pool their money and professional portfolio managers buy a collection of real estate investments. Some REITs buy properties such as apartments, office buildings, shopping centers, and hotels. Others invest in mortgage loans. A few are hybrid REITs, investing in a combination of properties and mortgages. REITs tend to pay relatively high dividends, making them good income investments. And since they trade on major exchanges, they can be liquidated at any time. Choose a REIT as you would a mutual fund: Look at the underlying assets and the track record of the portfolio manager.

CHAPTER ELEVEN

Paid Employment

Work is more fun than fun.

—Noel Coward

We put paid employment last in this section on sources of income during retirement because although you may want to work during retirement, you probably won't want to be doing it for the money. Most retirees see postretirement careers as something they do for fun and a challenge. They see retirement as a time to explore new fields of endeavor, a time to operate under a different set of rules from the ones they had to follow when they were obligated to support themselves and their families by bringing home a regular paycheck. The prevailing mood among retirees is that if you have to go to a job every day because you need the money—well, that's not retirement at all.

When planning ahead for retirement, it can be dangerous to count on income from work. For one thing, you never know how you'll feel about working in "retirement" until you get there. You could be so burned out after a forty-year nonstop career that you'll never want to see a paycheck again as long as

you live. And though postretirement careers can seem glamorous and fun when you're locked into a job you can't wait to
get out of, you may find they're not all they're cracked up to be
once you get into the day-to-day realities of the work itself.

Another thing to remember is that the energy and enthusi-
asm you have for working when you're in your 60s and 70s may
lose steam and fizzle out entirely when you get into your 80s. So
if your retirement bucket is low to start, meaning that you must
work in order to support yourself, you should count on that
income for only a limited period of time. And if at all possible,
you should take part of each paycheck and add it to your retirement bucket to prepare for the day when you'll be quitting
work for good.

This is not to discourage you from working during retirement. Far from it. In fact, this chapter is designed to get your
juices flowing and encourage you to think about the many
ways you can enrich your life by working at something you really
love. Consider the opportunities discussed in this chapter as
you would any other hobby or interest: Is it something you'd get
a charge out of and that would keep you vibrant and alive during the last third of your life? If so, don't let the fact that you'll
be getting paid for it deter you from pursuing an activity you
enjoy.

WHY WORK?

We hope that all of our talk about planning for a long life
expectancy will help make it a reality. We really do believe
that attitude has a lot to do with it. If you *want* to live a long
time, and you *expect* to live a long time, and you have enough
money to live a long time, you probably *will* live a long time. You
could easily live as long as twenty or thirty or forty years past
your normal retirement age. What will you do for all those many
years?

The best part about working after retirement is that you are
doing it on your terms. This is especially true if you don't need
the money. Just knowing you have the ability to say "Take this

job and shove it" (in a polite way, of course) means you will never have to settle for poor working conditions or a boss you can't stand. If you view work as a stimulating activity that gives you just as much pleasure as a favorite hobby—with the added dimension of fulfillment because you are contributing a part of yourself to the world—you can completely redefine the notion of work. Work becomes play, and play becomes work, and when you really get absorbed in it, you can't tell the difference.

So what are some of the reasons you might want to work during retirement?

- **Money**—Okay, we can't deny it. The money is nice, even if you don't need it. Take an extra vacation, put it in trust for your grandchildren, give it away to charity. Or just add it to your retirement bucket to provide an extra cushion for later.

- **Social interaction**—One of the hardest parts about retiring is not seeing the old gang at work every day. Workplace relationships are different from other social relationships because they're with people you may not go out of your way to get together with, yet you really do enjoy their company. Working gives you an opportunity to interact with people with whom you have a common bond.

- **Meaning and purpose**—There are probably studies supporting this, but we would suspect that people who have no purpose in life tend to die sooner. Working—even at the most basic kinds of jobs—provides meaning and purpose and a reason to keep on living.

- **Relief from boredom**—Not all retirees get pleasure from hobbies. If you find yourself flitting from one activity to another without finding satisfaction in any of them, what you may need is a job. Working puts structure in your day and gives you something concrete to do with your time.

WHAT KIND OF WORK DO YOU WANT TO DO?

The real beauty in working after retirement is that the sky's the limit. You can completely redefine the work experience and do something totally different from the career that occupied half your life. Or you can take that long-standing career—and all the skills that go with it—and reshape it to fit your new retirement lifestyle. Here are some possibilities for postretirement work.

START A NEW CAREER

Some people take this opportunity to dive into a new career with the same ambition—if not more—that they had when they were in their 20s. It's not unusual today to see older people on college campuses or in vocational training courses who are serious about learning new skills so they can start new careers. If you've always had a managerial or other white-collar job, you may now want to work with your hands, doing carpentry, automotive repair, or piano tuning. If your previous career required analytical skills, you may choose to exercise the right side of your brain by studying graphic design, interior decorating, or flower arranging. Although it takes a fair amount of drive and motivation, starting a new career could be one of the most rewarding things you'll do in retirement. It's a fresh start. Not only do you get to realize your dreams and curiosities, but you get to do it with no strings attached. If it turns out that you're not as good at something as you thought you'd be, all you have to do is pick something different and start over. This time around, the only person you have to answer to is yourself.

Examining Yourself, Your Qualities, and the Things You Like to Do

You know those aptitude tests you took in high school that told you if you should be a forest ranger or a teacher? Well, you may want to take them again. You're a different person now, with different skills and interests than you had when you were 18. Plus, the world is different today. Many of today's careers didn't even exist back then. Here are some other ways to assess your interests:

- **Conduct a self-test.** Ask friends, family members, ex-bosses, co-workers what they think are your best qualities and what sort of career might suit you. Sometimes the people around us are our best resource for discovering such information because they understand our needs and desires and are always looking out for our best interests. Also, they can tell us (with grace and understanding) what we don't want to hear.

- **Take a skills and personality test.** These tests are usually administered by career counselors, college career counseling centers, and some nonprofit groups (at no charge). There are literally hundreds of tests on the market, but two of the most popular ones are the Myers-Briggs Type Indicator and the Strong Interest Inventory. Each test can be completed in an hour or less.

- **Go to your favorite library or bookstore.** Several resources in print can help you determine what your skills and personality traits are and how you can best use them in a career setting. The classic *What Color Is Your Parachute?* by Richard Bolles (Ten-Speed Press, 1997) has come to be known as a career bible. It's full of time-tested wisdom on changing jobs and rethinking careers and includes specific information on how to work with a career counselor.

- **Contact your local university or community college.** The placement center at your local university or college may be of some help, as may the alumni association of your alma mater. College counseling centers offer skill and personality tests and can steer you in the right direction for courses on career development.

- **Seek professional career counseling.** Private counselors typically charge $75 to $150 an hour for guidance in career planning and for administering and interpreting tests. You won't be able to get all the information you need in just an hour, but four or five visits should do. Call the National Board for Certified Counselors (800-398-5389) in Greensboro, North Carolina, for the names of practitioners in your area. The NBCC will provide a free list of certified counselors in your area.

Getting the Training You Need

The amount of education and training you need will depend on how far you plan to wander from your current line of work. If you want to start a home-based word processing business, a few computer courses may be all you'll need. If you decide to fulfill a lifelong dream of becoming a lawyer, you know you're in for at least three years of full-time schooling, in addition to the grueling process of taking entrance exams and applying to law schools.

When exploring education and training resources, look for schools that provide the right kind of education for the career you have in mind. In addition to regular degree-granting programs, there are many professional courses and certificate programs offered through university extension programs or vocational schools. Libraries, bookstores, college recruiters, and the Internet are all good resources for the college-bound.

Whatever career you end up pursuing, computer literacy is practically essential these days. If you feel like the world is passing you by because you don't know how to operate a computer, sign up for classes offered through your local college or private learning company.

Finding a Job

The good news about postretirement careers is that employers are hiring people like you. Employers understand that 50+ workers have the skills, life experience, and knowledge to do the job and are generally more dependable than younger workers. Some companies have even begun hiring back older employees they laid off years ago in order to reclaim a precious resource that can't be found in younger workers.

Networking will put you in touch with the right people in the right circles to help you find the job you're looking for. By reaching out to the many people you know—and the many people they know—you can tap into the vast hidden employment market consisting of job openings that never show up in the classifieds or even on a recruiter's computer list. Many companies today rely on personal referrals to find their employees rather than publicizing them through traditional avenues.

Also consider conducting informational interviews with people in your field. These are informal discussions with influential people who are willing to impart some of their knowledge and advice to someone getting started in a career. The key to success with informational interviews is not to ask for a job from people you are interviewing. Simply let them know you are available and ask if they know of anyone looking for someone with your skills and attributes.

Reshape Your Current Career

Does the idea of starting a whole new career make you tired just thinking about it? That's okay. Nobody says you have to do it. Remember, working in retirement is something you do for yourself, not somebody else. New careers are for people with burning desires and lots of energy. Maybe you'd just rather take the skills and experience you do have and create a work situation that is easy to manage and provides the level of fulfillment you desire.

Go Part-Time

Many employers now see the value of part-time jobs and flexible work schedules in meeting their staffing needs. If you can convince an employer (maybe the one you just left?) that the only way to take advantage of your vast storehouse of skills and experience is to hire you part time, they just might do it. With more and more companies open to the idea of telecommuting, you may even be able to do some of your work at home in your slippers.

Go Freelance

Instead of working for just one employer, work for lots of them—only call them "clients" now. Consulting is a natural progression in a retiree's work life because it allows you to choose your projects and work whenever you want. With all the experience you gained in your previous career, you should have no trouble selling your services to your former boss as well as to companies you once thought of as competitors. All you need to get started are a couple of phone lines, a fax machine, a computer with e-mail capabilities, and a desk. Depending on how aggressively you want to market yourself, you may also need business cards plus a brochure or marketing kit.

Go Temp

Temporary employment is similar to consulting in that it offers variety and flexibility. The main difference is that you don't need to market yourself or hustle for projects. Instead, you go where the temp agency sends you, and usually work on-site. Although temp work has long been popular for administrative or clerical workers, some temp agencies work with mid- to senior-level managers. Contact a few employment agencies in your area to see if they have the need for someone with your skills.

START A NEW BUSINESS

Have you always wanted to be your own boss? Do you have an idea for a business that you just know will succeed? Do you have a hobby that could easily be turned into a moneymaking venture? If so, then you've probably thought about starting your own business. As you may know, starting a new business is no easy proposition. But that's not why people do it. There's a drive, a passion, an energy, that grips the entrepreneur and forces him or her to do certain irrational things, like dump a bunch of money into a venture that has no assurance of success and stay up till three o'clock in the morning working for weeks on end. Entrepreneurial zeal is a mysterious force. You either have it or you don't. If you have it and the people around you don't, they'll tell you you're crazy. But you know you're not. You have a vision that you are determined to make real, and you will do whatever it takes to make that happen.

Since we do not want you emptying your retirement bucket on a venture that could leave you destitute in your old age, we must inject the voice of reason here (knowing full well that if you're determined to make your endeavor fly, you'll ignore our advice and do whatever you want to do). The most important piece of advice we can offer is to be careful. Unless you have a very full retirement bucket, you are not in a position to be taking excessive risks at this stage of your life. A new business can be a money pit, and once you start pouring money into it, you can find your retirement bucket depleted before you even know what happened. And once you're retired, you do not have the means to make it back. That said, a postretirement business can be a wonderful way to keep you involved and make some extra money.

The Benefits of Owning Your Own Business

Every entrepreneur has a different reason for starting a business. Some have a fantastic idea and a burning passion to get it to market. Others are looking for a new lifestyle that goes with running a particular kind of business, such as traveling with craft shows. Others simply want to bring in a little extra money and work whenever they want. People who own their own business say there's absolutely nothing like it, especially after the initial hurdles have been crossed and the business is thriving on its own momentum. Some of the reasons successful entrepreneurs give for loving what they do are the following:

- **You are in control.** Nobody tells you what to do or when to do it (except your customers, of course). You can work early in the morning or late at night. You can hire other people to do the tasks you don't want to do. You can work a few hours a day or none at all. For many entrepreneurs, the most important aspect of owning a business is the ability to be in control and be their own boss.

- **You can take pride in your work.** When you own the business, you can impose your own quality standards on the product or service being offered. You never have to settle for less than what you really want. And there is great satisfaction in working with customers who not only appreciate your product or service but actually pay for it.

- **You reap the profits.** If you've been accustomed to receiving a regular paycheck every two weeks, owning a business will expose you to the exhilaration (and terror) of receiving undetermined amounts at unpredictable times. If your business is a fantastic success, you could make more money than you ever thought possible. On the other hand . . .

The Drawbacks of Owning a Business

If you see entrepreneurship as nothing but a glamorous endeavor that will make you rich with very little effort, you probably should spend some time exploring the realities of business ownership. Visit your local dry cleaner or independent hardware store and talk to the owner about how long it took to build up the business. Better yet, talk to people who already own the type of business you're interested in starting and ask them to be honest with you about how much time they put in (both in the beginning and now that the business is a going concern), and if they would do it all over again. It's important not to let yourself become discouraged by other people's negative experiences, but you may learn some things that will help you decide if entrepreneurship really is right for you. Here are some of the drawbacks you may hear about:

- **It's risky.** If you have grand aspirations for your business, you will need lots of capital, whether it comes from your own retirement bucket or you take out loans using your house or other assets as collateral. Even if you start your new business on a shoestring, you'll need to put some money into it, and there's no assurance that you will see a return on your investment.

- **It can be confining.** You know that freedom and control we talked about above under benefits? Well, there's another side to it. Once your business is up and running, it can be terribly confining due to customer commitments and the reality that no one can run your business as well as you.

- **It can be emotionally grueling.** When your business is your "baby," you can't help becoming emotionally involved. As your business goes through its normal cycles, you will celebrate or despair as appropriate, riding an emotional roller coaster that can be both fun and terrifying. One thing is for sure. You won't be bored.

Do You Have What It Takes to Be an Entrepreneur?

Here are some of the traits of successful entrepreneurs. How many of them do you have?

- **Drive.** Customers will not come knocking on your door. You have to get out and hustle if you're going to get your products or services sold.

- **Confidence.** You have to really believe your product or service is valuable and needed, and then be able to talk about it with conviction.

- **Determination.** Starting a new business is no piece of cake. You must be able to stick with it even when you are seeing little progress.

- **Integrity.** You must stand behind your business and be seen by clients as honest and trustworthy.

- **Experience.** It helps to have some knowledge of the business you are getting into. Even if you don't have all the answers, you need to know how to find them.

- **Common sense.** Your business instincts must be grounded in reality.

- **Flexibility.** You must be flexible enough to be able to go on to another idea if the first one doesn't work.

Steps to Take

If all you want to do is convert your hobby into a business and the profit motive is low on your list of goals, there's nothing to keep you from diving right in and starting to charge for the things you used to do for free. But if you have more ambitious goals requiring significant investments of time and capital, you'll need to do some careful planning. Here are some of the steps you'll need to take.

- **Do your research.** There's a lot that goes into starting a business, and you need to know what you're getting into before you accelerate full throttle. If you've always had a passion for making kites, for example, you need to make sure there's a market for them, that you know how to produce them en masse, and that you know how to get them into the hands of the people who will buy them.

- **Study the competition.** Knowing what your competitors are doing is critical to knowing how to make, price, market, and sell your product or service effectively. Study your competitors' products, prices, services, and distribution channels so you can not only get ideas but differentiate your business from the competition.

- **Develop a plan.** You'll need some kind of plan to get you started and keep you on course as you go along. Write down your business objectives, how you plan to market your product or service to customers, and why they would buy it.

GET A PART-TIME JOB

If you don't want to go all out and start a new career or business, and if you have no interest in continuing with your present career even in a reduced capacity, maybe the answer is to get a part-time job doing something you like. If you've always liked books, you could get a job in a library or bookstore. If you're into gardening, you could work part time at your local nursery. If you like fixing things around the house, consider becoming a part-time handyman or work at your local hardware store. If you like social interaction, work in a pub or coffeehouse. When exploring potential part-time jobs, use your imagination; do not rely on classified ads or "help wanted" signs in store windows as your only options.

First, think about what you like to do. What stores do you like to shop in? What do you like to do in your spare time? If you could have any job in the world, what would it be? Next, think about the more practical aspects of working, such as how far you're willing to drive and what hours would be acceptable to you. And finally, get out and talk to people about job possibilities. If an employer doesn't have a specific opening for part-time help, you may be able to convince him or her to hire you anyway. After all, you have the skills, the desire, and the work ethic to make an excellent employee. Who wouldn't want to hire you?

FINANCIAL IMPLICATIONS OF WORKING

Regardless of what kind of job, career, or business you end up pursuing, there will be certain financial implications which you'll need to factor into your plan.

WORK-RELATED EXPENSES

Work-related expenses could range from nothing to an elaborate home office setup to a major investment in tools and equipment. Before jumping into your postretirement job or career, be sure to estimate all of your anticipated work-related expenses and factor these into your budget. In addition to the initial expenses, don't forget the little things that add up over time, like clothes, gasoline, and lunches out.

INCOME TAXES

You will, of course, have to pay income taxes on any wages or profits you receive from your employer or your business. But don't let that keep you from working. The government never takes 100 percent of your income, so you'll always end up with more in your pocket by working as compared to not working. In fact, you may be able to turn the tables and make the tax rules work in your favor. If you turn your hobby into a business, for example, you may be able to deduct some of your current out-of-pocket expenses, even if you don't turn a profit right away. (Be sure to check the IRS rules on hobby-related businesses.) If working will put you into a higher tax bracket, you'll want to consider what it will do to the rest of your financial plan and adjust your investment strategy, if necessary.

REDUCTION IN SOCIAL SECURITY BENEFITS

As we pointed out in Chapter 7, if you are under age 70, your Social Security benefits may be reduced if you work. If you are between the ages of 62 and 64 and earn more than the earnings limitation ($9,600 in 1999), your Social Security benefit will be reduced by $1 for every $2 over the limit that you earn. If you are between the ages of 65 and 69 and earn more than the earnings limitation for your age group ($15,500 in 1999), your benefits will be reduced by $1 for each $3 over the limit that you earn. After age 70 there is no reduction in benefits regardless of how much you earn.

ABILITY TO CONTRIBUTE TO IRAs

If you want to keep contributing to your retirement bucket and get the tax benefits of IRAs, you'll need to work in order to do it. Earned income is a requirement for making IRA contributions, but it doesn't take much. The law says you can contribute up to 100 percent of your salary up to $2,000. So if you earn just $1,000 in a year, you can contribute $1,000 to an IRA; if you make $2,000, you can make the full contribution. Remember that if you are over 70½, you may not contribute to a regular IRA, but you may still contribute to a Roth IRA.

PART
FOUR

Where It Goes

CHAPTER TWELVE

Taxes

The hardest thing in the world to
understand is the income tax.

—Albert Einstein

If you've managed to keep your financial life fairly simple during your working years, you probably haven't had to think too much about taxes. Just check a box on your W-2 form at work to indicate how much tax should be withheld from your paycheck, file your tax return every year by April 15, and you've done your patriotic duty. For most working people, the biggest issue with taxes is just getting them done—gathering up receipts, getting the forms filled out, and mailing them off by midnight on April 15. Other than this flurry of activity that takes place once a year, taxes are largely absent from their consciousness.

As you approach retirement, however, this blissful disregard of the joys and sorrows of our federal income tax system will have to change. Like it or not, you're going to have to become intimately familiar with the different kinds of income that are subject to taxes, and you'll need to do some advance planning to keep from paying more than your fair share to Uncle

Sam. The bottom line? You'll be thinking about taxes all year long—especially when making critical retirement planning decisions.

Before, all you had were wages, and your taxes were automatically withheld for you. Now you'll have lots of different kinds of income, and you'll be responsible for sending checks to the IRS. The irony here is that most people think their lives will become simpler after retirement. They assume that since their income will be lower, their taxes will be lower—and since there's not a lot they can do to reduce their tax bill anyway, why worry about it? But many retirees find just the opposite to be true. With so many financial decisions based on the after-tax consequences of various actions, tax planning becomes a crucial part of overall financial management. But the task is certainly not insurmountable. There's plenty of help out there, and once your retirement plan is in place, you'll be able to relax and focus on greens fees instead.

WHY YOUR TAX BILL MAY BE HIGHER <u>AFTER</u> YOU RETIRE

If you plan things right, you'll have a comfortable, financially secure retirement, with plenty of income to do the things you want to do and enough stashed away in savings and retirement accounts to last the rest of your life. And therein lies the rub. The more income you have, the more taxes you'll pay. And the more you have stashed away in IRAs and various retirement accounts, the more you'll have to take out—and pay taxes on— when you turn 70½. These are not reasons to give up and forget this whole retirement planning business. As mentioned earlier, the government never takes 100 percent of your income, so even though you'll be paying more in taxes, you'll still have more left in your pocket. But do take heed that taxes can consume a fairly large chunk of your income after you retire, for two simple reasons: (1) your income may stay the same or go up and (2) you may have fewer deductions.

Your Income May Stay the Same or Go Up

If you want to lead an active, involved life, you'll need enough income to support all those activities you have planned for yourself. When you're working, you don't have time to engage in a lot of travel, hobbies, and educational pursuits. You're too busy *making* money to have time to *spend* it. The opposite is true during retirement. You have nothing but time, and unless you plan to spend most of it working, either as a volunteer or in a paying job, whatever activities you choose probably will cost money. If you're still at the stage of retirement planning where you can decide how much income you want to have during retirement, be sure to factor in enough for taxes so you'll be left with the amount you need.

One thing you won't have a choice about is how much you must start taking out of your IRA accounts when you turn 70½. The more successful you are in accumulating and investing your IRA money, the more taxable income you'll have to report when you start taking minimum mandatory withdrawals. This is another reason why your income—and your tax bill—may stay the same or go up after you retire.

You May Have Fewer Deductions

In an effort to simplify your financial life and reduce your monthly expenses, you may decide to pay off your mortgage. There goes one big tax deduction. Your kids may finally grow up and leave the nest. There goes another. Once you leave your job, you will no longer be contributing to retirement plans. There goes another. So even if your income stays the same or goes down after retirement, your tax bill actually could go up because you'll have fewer deductions to offset the income. This is not to say that paying off your mortgage or kicking the kids out of the house is necessarily a bad thing. Just be aware of the tax consequences of your actions.

Income tax basics

Once again, we digress for the new people. If you've been doing your taxes for years and have a solid understanding of how our progressive income tax system works, you can skip this section or refer to it to explain financial matters to a loved one. On the other hand, if you've always been somewhat confused by tax matters and the extent of your involvement has been signing your name to a joint return that you couldn't explain if your life depended on it, read on.

WHAT'S TAXABLE AND WHAT'S NOT

The U.S. federal income tax system, passed by Congress in 1913, is our Treasury's biggest source of income. By paying a portion of your income to the federal government in taxes, you help support the many activities our government carries out for the health and well-being of its citizens. Besides, it's the law. Once a year, everyone with income over a certain amount must complete a tax form—called Form 1040—declaring how much income he or she received during the calendar year. But you don't have to pay taxes on all of your income. You can deduct from your *total* income certain expenses to arrive at your *taxable* income. Once you've determined your taxable income, you refer to a schedule published by the IRS that tells how much tax you owe. If you've already had at least that amount withheld from your paycheck during the year, you don't need to send the IRS a check—in fact, you may even get a refund. If the table says you owe more than the amount withheld, you'll have to send a check for the additional amount.

Now, this is an extremely simplified explanation of how our tax system works. The part about tax deductions—where you go from total income to taxable income—is the most complicated of all. There are hundreds—even thousands—of possible tax deductions that allow you to legally reduce your taxable income and pay less income tax, and that's a major part of tax planning. By carefully structuring the type and amount of income you receive during retirement, and by reducing it by all the deductions you are legally entitled to take, you achieve that critical balance that gives you the income you need without paying too much income tax.

First let's talk about what income is considered taxable and what is not.

Taxable Income That Must Be Reported

The following types of income must be declared on your 1040:

- Earned income (wages, salaries, tips, and some fringe benefits)
- Unearned income (interest, dividends, and capital gains)
- Self-employment (or partnership) income
- Real estate rental income
- Royalty, estate, and trust income
- Alimony income
- Pension income
- IRA income
- Unemployment and sick pay
- Strike benefits
- Gambling winnings
- Prizes, awards, and cash payments for services
- Barter income

Tax-Free Income You Don't Need to Report

- Welfare, veterans' disability, and workers' compensation benefits
- Supplemental security income (SSI) from Social Security
- Child support
- Gifts and inheritances
- Life insurance proceeds received after a death
- Scholarships for tuition, if you are studying for a degree
- Loan proceeds

Income That May Be Taxable

- Social Security benefits (taxable if your other income is substantial—covered later in this chapter)

- State and local income tax refunds (taxable if you deducted them in a previous year)

Income That Is Tax-Free but Must Be Shown on Your Return

- Interest from state and local municipal bonds

ADJUSTMENTS TO INCOME

The first step in going from *total* income to *taxable* income is to make certain adjustments. This step determines your *adjusted gross income* (AGI). Your adjusted gross income is an important figure to know because it determines your eligibility to do certain things, like contribute to a Roth IRA. Throughout this book and other financial materials you may come across, you may see phrases like "if your adjusted gross income (AGI) is less than $100,000 . . ." Without knowing what your own AGI is, the information that follows would be meaningless to you. So pull out a copy of your last 1040 and look on line 32 at the bottom of the first page, adjusted gross income, and memorize it. Now you'll be able to relate personally to rules and regulations having to do with AGI. The main adjustments that get you from total income to adjusted gross income are:

- Qualifying contributions to IRAs

- Contributions to Keogh and SEP retirement plans for the self-employed

- Alimony payments

- Qualified moving expenses

- Half of the self-employment tax

Needless to say, the more adjustments you have, the less your taxable income will be and the less tax you will pay. That's why we're always preaching to people about making contributions to IRAs and qualified retirement plans. Unlike other adjustments, such as alimony, moving expenses, and self-employment tax, contributions to IRAs and retirement plans are "expenses" you pay to yourself. In other words, you get to deduct them from your income for tax purposes, but the money is really yours to keep.

EXEMPTIONS AND DEDUCTIONS

Exemptions and deductions are items you subtract from your adjusted gross income to finally arrive at your taxable income. The personal exemption is a specific amount you get to subtract just for being alive. This amount is indexed for inflation and was $2,750 in 1999. Deductions are additional items you subtract from your adjusted gross income. These include things like:

- State and local taxes
- Interest payments on home mortgages and home equity loans
- Charitable contributions
- Unreimbursed medical and dental costs that exceed 7.5 percent of your AGI
- Casualty and theft losses
- Home office deduction
- Unreimbursed business expenses like meals, travel, and entertainment
- Certain education expenses

Without encouraging you to take deductions you're not entitled to, once again we'd like to remind you that the more deductions you take, the less tax you pay. If, after adding up all of your deductions, they do not total the *standard deduction* for your filing status (single, joint, or head of household), you can simply take the standard deduction and not worry about itemizing the various deductions. The standard deduction is indexed for inflation. In 1999 it was:

FILING STATUS	DEDUCTION
Married filing jointly and surviving spouses	$7,200
Married filing separately	$3,600
Head of household	$6,350
Single	$4,300

On the other hand, if you have lots of deductions and if your AGI is over a certain amount, your deductions will be reduced according to a formula too complicated to go into here. It seems Uncle Sam wants to make sure high-income people pay their fair share in taxes. He does this through various means, such as limiting tax deductions for high-income taxpayers and imposing the *alternative minimum tax*, which is *way* too complicated to go into here but which you should have an inkling of if you have high income and lots of tax deductions.

FIGURING THE TAX

Once you have entered your gross income, subtracted the adjustments to arrive at your adjusted gross income, and then subtracted the exemptions and deductions to arrive at your taxable income, you are ready to refer to the tax tables to find out how much tax you owe. This is one of those mechanical functions that most people let their accountants or computers do, but you can get hold of the IRS tax tables and actually look up, based on your taxable income and your filing status, how much tax you owe for the year. Once you know your base tax, you may be able to reduce it through tax credits. But since most tax credits are designed to help low-income people and families with children, most retirees are not eligible for them.

NUMBERS AND OTHER STUFF TO REMEMBER

There's a lot about taxes that you do *not* need to know or remember, either because it doesn't apply to you or because it's being taken care of by someone else, such as a spouse or accountant. But to understand the most basic aspects of tax planning, you should know and remember the following:

- **Your filing status,** whether single, married filing jointly, married filing separately, or head of household

- **Your adjusted gross income,** found on line 32 of Form 1040

- **Your taxable income,** found on line 38 of Form 1040

- **Your marginal tax rate** (see below)

UNDERSTANDING YOUR MARGINAL TAX RATE

Your *marginal tax rate*—also referred to as your *tax bracket*—is the most helpful piece of information you can have when doing tax planning. It tells you what percentage of your last dollar of income will be paid out in taxes. This, in turn, allows you to evaluate the wisdom of various financial strategies. For example, let's say you are married, file a joint return, and your taxable income during retirement is $30,000. That puts you in the 15 percent tax bracket. If you were thinking about working during retirement and wanted to know how much of your paycheck would be lost to taxes, you'd simply multiply your expected wages by 15 percent and subtract it from the original amount to arrive at your after-tax income. So let's say you were thinking about taking a job that paid $12,000 a year. Fifteen percent of $12,000 is $1,800. Subtract $1,800 from $12,000 and you get an after-tax income of $10,200. You can use this number when planning your budget.

But what if you were thinking of taking a job that paid $18,000 a year? Well, in this case that would put you into a higher bracket. If you add $18,000 to your current $30,000, your income would total $48,000, or $5,649 more than the $42,351 cutoff for the 15 percent bracket for married people filing jointly. This means that the $18,000 in potential wages would be taxed at two rates. The first $12,351 would be taxed at 15 percent and the remaining $5,649 would be taxed at 28 percent, leaving you with after-tax income of $14,596 (plus your $30,000 from other sources). Now you can decide if you want to take the job after all, knowing that Uncle Sam will get $3,404 of your hard-earned $18,000.

To see what your marginal tax rate is, refer to Table 12.1. By the way, these tax rates apply to federal income tax only. If you live in a state that has a state income tax, you'll want to factor it in as well.

How taxes affect your
retirement planning decisions

Corporate Pension

If you've never worried much about taxes before, just wait until you are faced with the prospect of receiving a six- or seven-digit retirement distribution. Take it all in one year and the taxes on that baby would build a couple of bridges and a few high-explosive warheads. Okay, we're kidding about the bridges and the warheads, but we're dead serious about the possibility of losing a huge chunk of your retirement distribution to taxes. And once it's gone, it's gone. That's why we harped ad nauseum in Chapter 8 about taking your retirement distribution in a lump sum (rather than an annuity) and putting it immediately into an IRA rollover account to avoid paying taxes on the distribution. Considering all the other tax decisions you'll be making, this is an easy one.

Not so easy are the decisions that require predicting the future—like what your tax bracket will be in ten or twenty years. Not only is your future income a mystery, but the tax rates themselves could change between now and then. Also difficult are those decisions that hinge on others. For example, if you're thinking about going back to work, you'll need to factor in how your wages will affect your Social Security benefits, which may in turn influence your decision about when to apply for Social Security in the first place. But like a dog chasing its tail, at some point these circular issues will offer an opening that will allow you to sit down and sort everything all out.

TABLE 12.1   1999 TAX RATE SCHEDULE

TAXABLE INCOME ($)	BASE AMOUNT OF TAX ($)		RATE ON EXCESS	OF THE AMOUNT OVER ($)
SINGLE				
0 to 25,750	0	+	15.0%	0
25,750 to 62,450	3,862.50	+	28.0%	25,750
62,450 to 130,250	14,138.50	+	31.0%	62,450
130,250 to 283,150	35,156.50	+	36.0%	130,250
Over 283,150	90,200.50	+	39.6%	283,150
HEAD OF HOUSEHOLD				
0 to 34,550	0	+	15.0%	0
34,550 to 89,150	5,182.50	+	28.0%	34,550
89,150 to 144,400	20,470.50	+	31.0%	89,150
144,400 to 283,150	37,598.00	+	36.0%	144,400
Over 283,150	87,548.00	+	39.6%	283,150
MARRIED FILING JOINTLY AND SURVIVING SPOUSES				
0 to 43,050	0	+	15.0%	0
43,050 to 104,050	6,457.50	+	28.0%	43,050
104,050 to 158,550	23,537.50	+	31.0%	104,050
158,550 to 283,150	40,432.50	+	36.0%	158,550
Over 283,150	85,288.50	+	39.6%	283,150
MARRIED FILING SEPARATELY				
0 to 21,525	0	+	15.0%	0
21,525 to 52,025	3,228.75	+	28.0%	21,525
52,025 to 79,275	11,768.75	+	31.0%	52,025
79,275 to 141,575	20,215.25	+	36.0%	79,275
Over 141,575	42,644.25	+	39.6%	141,575

Social Security

Social Security benefits are normally not taxable, unless your *combined income* is over a certain amount. Now, so far we've talked about *total* income, *adjusted gross* income, and *taxable* income. What in the world is *combined* income? This is a special term used for calculating the tax on Social Security benefits. It is the sum of your adjusted gross income plus any nontaxable interest income (such as interest from municipal bonds) plus one-half of your Social Security benefits. If your combined income is over the first threshold indicated below, you'll pay taxes on 50 percent of your Social Security benefits. If your combined income is over the second threshold, you'll pay taxes on up to 85 percent of your Social Security benefits.

Here are the thresholds: If you are married filing jointly, the first threshold is $32,000, the second is $44,000. If you are filing as a single taxpayer, the first threshold is $25,000, the second is $34,000. And get this: If you are married filing separately, the threshold is *zero*, which means you'll probably have to pay taxes on your Social Security benefits no matter what your combined income is. (This is why many retirees choose to live together and file tax returns as single individuals rather than face the various marriage penalties older people are subject to.)

Every January you will receive a Social Security Benefit Statement (Form SSA-1099) in the mail showing the amount of benefits you received in the previous year. This, along with the number on line 32 (adjusted gross income) of your regular 1040, plus statements showing the amount of municipal bond interest you received during the year, will enable you to calculate your combined income for Social Security tax purposes.

Individual Retirement Accounts

If we'd written this book fifteen years ago, all we'd have to say about taxes and IRA distributions is that they're always taxable as ordinary income. Period. But in the mid-1980s Congress started monkeying around with IRAs and changed the rules so that some people were no longer allowed to make tax-deductible IRA contributions. They could, however, make nondeductible contributions. This changed the makeup of the money in the accounts. The part consisting of the nondeductible contribution (on which taxes had already been paid) would come out tax-free, while the part consisting of investment earnings (which had built up tax-free) would be fully taxable at distribution. If you have never in your lifetime made a nondeductible contribution to an IRA, do not clutter your brain with the preceding information. If you have, good luck figuring out how your IRA distributions will be taxed. Get some help with this because the calculations are complicated.

The other monkey wrench regarding the taxation of IRA distributions is the relatively new Roth IRA, whose distributions are always tax-free (unless the law changes between now and the time you're ready to take your money out). We covered the Roth IRA in Chapter 9, and there's not much more to say about it here except that it can be an excellent source of tax free income later in life.

INVESTMENT ACCOUNTS

Investment income that is not sheltered by an IRA or some other type of retirement account is taxable in the year it is received. This adds another layer of responsibility onto the management of your investment account. With a taxable account you must not only maximize investment returns, you must do it in a way that minimizes taxes. Fortunately, there are several ways to do this:

- Carefully time your purchases and sales
- Minimize interest and dividend income
- Invest in tax-free municipal bonds
- Be careful with mutual funds
- Buy tax-advantaged investments

Carefully Time Your Purchases and Sales

If you buy a stock and sell it at a higher price less than a year later, you'll pay tax on the gain at your regular income tax rate.

(See Table 12.1) If you hold it at least twelve months, you'll pay tax at the long-term capital gains rate, maximum 20 percent (10 percent if you're in the 15 percent tax bracket). The important thing to remember about capital gains is not just that you pay less tax if you hold the asset at least a year but that you are not taxed at all until you sell it. This gives you enormous flexibility in managing your portfolio. If you don't want a taxable gain, don't sell the asset. (Of course, by the time you are ready to sell it the gain could turn into a loss, but that's the risk you run with capital assets.) Another nifty thing you can do with capital assets is to offset gains with losses. If you have both winners and losers in your portfolio, sell some of each. The losses will offset all or part of the gains and reduce your taxes. (This is a great way to clean house and get rid of losers you keep hoping will come back.) If you have more losses than gains, you can offset up to $3,000 of other taxable income in one year. And if you have a really bad year, you can carry forward losses of $3,000 a year until the tax deduction is exhausted.

Minimize Interest and Dividend Income

Interest and dividends are taxed at your regular income tax rate. (See Table 12.1.) To minimize this type of income, you can invest in low-dividend-paying stocks and avoid buying bonds altogether. Of course, taxes are not the only thing to consider when managing an investment portfolio. Stocks that don't pay dividends tend to be riskier than those that do, and bonds can add welcome stability to a portfolio of growth stocks even though the interest income is fully taxable. Again, taxes are just one element of portfolio management; you also have to consider your risk tolerance, time horizon, and income needs.

Invest in Tax-Free Municipal Bonds

The interest on municipal bonds is free from federal income tax and also free from state income tax if they are issued in the state where you live. Because of their tax-free status, the interest rate on municipal bonds is lower than for taxable bonds of the same quality and maturity, the theory being that the after-tax yield is the same for both. However, whether this is true or not depends on your tax bracket, which ought to be at least 31 percent before you even consider buying municipal bonds (and even then it's not a sure thing). It's best to do the calculations using real yields and your actual combined state and federal tax bracket before deciding to buy munis. And remember, municipal bond interest is used in the calculation of "combined income" for determining tax on Social Security benefits.

Be Careful with Mutual Funds

When you buy a mutual fund, you are precluded from doing any fancy tax strategies because you're not the one managing the portfolio. You pretty much have to take the taxable income they give you, whether you want it or not. There are a couple of things you can watch out for, however. First, buy a fund that has low turnover. (This information is in the prospectus or the fund's annual report.) If there's not a lot of buying and selling going on, there will be less short-term capital gains income. Second, before you invest, find out when a fund intends to make a big distribution, and wait until after the distribution to buy the shares. Do this so you won't be taxed on what is essentially your own money. Most funds make their biggest distributions around the end of the calendar year, so if you're planning on buying fund shares between September and December, call the fund and ask when it's safe to invest to avoid receiving the distribution.

Buy Tax-Advantaged Investments

Tax-managed mutual funds are specially designed to keep taxable income to a minimum. They do this by holding stocks for a long period of time and by concentrating on stocks that pay low or no dividends. In other words, tax-managed mutual funds manage the portfolio the same way you would if you were managing your own investments with an eye toward tax reduction.

Annuities are another popular tax-advantaged investment. An annuity works like a mutual fund in an IRA account. In other words, it's a professionally managed portfolio of securities whose investment earnings are not taxed until you take the money out. Annuities are actually life insurance products— that's what gives them their tax-favored status—but people buy them for the growth potential and tax benefits, not the life insurance aspect. There are many types of annuities on the market, so shop carefully and make sure you understand all the withdrawal provisions, including any penalties that may apply.

REAL ESTATE INCOME

Thanks to the Taxpayer Relief Act of 1997, it's unlikely you'll ever have to worry about paying capital gains tax when you sell your house. If you're single, you can exclude up to $250,000 in gains from taxes; if you're married filing jointly, you can exclude up to $500,000. The only catch is that you must have owned the home as your principal residence for two out of the last five years. It doesn't matter how old you are, you don't have to buy another home to get this exclusion, and you can do it as many times as you want, as long as you meet the two-year ownership rule.

Other real estate income opportunities discussed in Chapter 10 have varying tax implications. Reverse mortgages provide income that is completely tax free and do not affect Social Security benefits. Sale-leasebacks and ownership of income property have serious tax implications, so be sure to get professional help before entering into one of these arrangements.

PAID EMPLOYMENT

Of all the different types of taxable income, employment income is the one you're most familiar with because you've been dealing with it for so many years. Just remember that employment income affects Social Security benefits in two ways: Between the ages of 62 and 69, it reduces actual benefits (refer to Chapter 7), and at any age it figures into the income that determines whether your Social Security benefits will be taxed. On the other hand, you need to have earned income if you want to keep contributing to a Roth IRA to ensure a source of tax-free income in your old age.

We believe that working during retirement can provide such fulfillment and satisfaction that the decision to work should be based on reasons other than taxes. If you want to work, work. Consider the taxes a small price to pay for being a productive American citizen.

OTHER TAXES

In addition to income tax, other types of taxes include sales tax, property tax, and estate and gift tax. There's not a lot you can do about sales tax except refrain from buying taxable items or move to a state that has no sales tax, like Oregon. Property taxes relate to housing decisions. Estate and gift taxes will be covered in Chapter 16.

CHAPTER THIRTEEN

Insurance

*Happiness has many roots, but none
more important than security.*

—Edward R. Stettinius, Jr.

Insurance premiums can take another large bite out of your budget when you're retired. It's easy to get carried away with insurance because the benefits sound so attractive: "You mean, if I die my heirs will get $1 million? Where do I sign?" or "What? Nursing home care costs $50,000 a year? I'd better buy some long-term care insurance while I'm still young and healthy."

The concept behind insurance is sound. Get lots of people to put small amounts of money into a big pot. Then if something happens to a few of those people, pay them the large sums they're entitled to (after the insurance company takes its cut, of course) and remind the people who don't get anything back how lucky they are that nothing bad happened to them. Of course, if too many people file a claim against the pot, the system fails. That's why we depend on insurance companies to manage the pot properly so we'll be assured that should we ever need it, God forbid, the money will be there.

When you buy insurance, you are transferring risk: the risk you'll get sick and need a costly operation . . . the risk that you'll die and leave a spouse with no means of support . . . the risk that your car will be damaged in an accident . . . the risk that your house will burn down. These are major life risks. Fortunately, they don't happen to too many people. That's how insurance companies can charge (sometimes) reasonable premiums and stay in business: Lots of people pay in, few people take out.

But as good a deal as insurance sounds, we want you to use your judgment when buying it. When you pay insurance premiums, you are out-of-pocket that money. In other words, the risk is 100 percent that you will lose whatever money you pay out in premiums. Now, if the peace of mind you get in exchange for that expenditure is worth it to you, go ahead and keep paying. But if you are paying premiums out of habit, or because somebody convinced you it's "the right thing to do," we encourage you to reexamine your insurance purchases and decide whether (1) you really need the insurance, and (2) you really need this type and amount of insurance from this particular company. It is normal and natural to want to transfer risk as you get older, especially when you have a lot to lose. But insurance companies are notorious for selling to people's emotions, so you'll feel good about paying into this pot that you never (you hope) get anything back from. Don't buy into the emotion. Instead, evaluate insurance as a financial proposition, decide if the transfer of risk is worth the premiums you'll have to pay, and shop around for the best deal.

HEALTH INSURANCE

One of the most important matters you'll have to take care of when you leave your company for good is to make sure your health insurance continues without interruption. As you enter the maze of health insurance options, you will come to appreciate the passage of COBRA, which is the Consolidated Omnibus Budget Reconciliation Act of 1985, the law that made it mandatory for employers to let departing employees continue their health care coverage (at their own expense) for at least eighteen months. Although it is not a permanent solution and you will have to pay the premiums yourself, COBRA buys you some time to shop around for the best health care coverage for yourself and your family.

Some employers offer ongoing health benefits to retirees as part of their retirement package. This could be a really good deal—or it could leave you stuck if your employer reduces or cancels coverage in the future. Here's how to find out: Get a copy of your employer's plan document, called the summary plan description (SPD). If you see language such as "The company reserves the right to modify, revoke, suspend, terminate, or change the program, in whole or in part, at any time," that's a pretty clear message that you could find yourself scrambling for health insurance just when you need it the most. Consider your employer's insurance as one option available to you and start becoming an expert on the various kinds of health insurance available in the marketplace.

Understanding Medicare

Although you may not yet be eligible for Medicare when you leave your job, it's important to understand what you will be entitled to—and when—so you can integrate Medicare with your existing insurance when you turn 65. Medicare has undergone some changes recently to give people more options for increasing their coverage, since the original plan left so many gaps in coverage. Now you have three choices: (1) Stick with the original Medicare (and all of its limitations), (2) take the original Medicare and buy a supplemental insurance policy to cover the gaps, and (3) enroll in a Medicare managed care plan. The next sections discuss each of these options.

The Original Medicare Plan

The original Medicare is composed of two parts. Part A is the hospital insurance portion, which covers inpatient hospital care, skilled nursing care, home health care, and hospice care. You become eligible for Medicare Part A at age 65. If you are already receiving Social Security, you will automatically be enrolled in Part A and will receive your Medicare card three months before your sixty-fifth birthday. If you have not yet applied for Social Security benefits, you will need to apply for Medicare Part A, and you should go ahead and do so three months before your sixty-fifth birthday, even if: (1) you are still working, (2) will continue to be covered by your employer's health plan, or (3) plan to delay taking Social Security benefits. Unlike delaying Social Security benefits, there's no advantage to waiting to apply for Part A Medicare. Part A is free if you are eligible for Social Security benefits based on your own or your spouse's work history (even if you haven't started collecting benefits yet), or if you or your spouse worked at least ten years in Medicare-covered employment; otherwise you must pay a monthly premium of either $170 or $309, depending on how many quarters of coverage you have.

Part A helps pay for up to 90 days of hospital care per *benefit period*. (A benefit period begins on the day you enter the hospital and ends 60 days after you leave.) During the first 60 days of hospitalization, Medicare pays all covered costs except the deductible of $768. On days 61 through 90, you must pay a coinsurance amount of $192 per day. If you want a private room or a TV or telephone, you have to pay extra. Part A also covers up to 90 days of skilled nursing facility care, home health care, and hospice care.

Part B is the medical insurance portion, which covers doctor bills, outpatient hospital care, and medical services and supplies like X rays. You become eligible for Part B Medicare at the same time you become eligible for Part A. But Part B is not free. You must pay a monthly premium ($45.50 in 1999), which, if you are receiving Social Security, is automatically deducted from your check. If you are still working or otherwise covered by an employer-sponsored plan, you'll want to decline Part B because you won't get much benefit from Medicare if your employer is the primary insurer. (You must specifically decline Part B if you don't want it.) Even worse, signing up for Part B triggers the beginning of the six-month Medigap open enrollment period (discussed below), and if you let this period go by, you could have a hard time getting supplemental medical insurance when your employer-sponsored coverage eventually runs out. If you have no other coverage or if you'll be switching insurers when you become eligible for Medicare, go ahead and sign up for Part B. (It's automatic when you sign up for Part A unless you specifically tell them you don't want it.)

Part B has significant limitations. It does not cover most prescription drugs, dental care, most immunization shots (it does cover flu and pneumonia shots), routine checkups and tests (it does cover Pap smears and mammograms), or nursing home care. In addition to paying a deductible of $100 per year, you must pay for whatever portion of the bill Medicare does not pay for. Medicare pays 80 percent of the *Medicare-approved amount*, so if your health care provider charges more than the Medicare-approved amount, you're stuck with the overage as well as the remaining 20 percent.

Original Medicare Plan with Supplemental Insurance Policy

If you like the traditional fee-for-service type of coverage (as opposed to managed care discussed next), you'll probably want to get a supplemental insurance policy—called *Medigap* insurance—to fill in the gaps left by Part A and B limitations. There are ten standard Medigap policies with letter designations ranging from A through J. Plan A is the basic benefit package; as you go up the alphabet the benefits increase, with Plan J providing the most coverage. Although the packages have been standardized, the premiums vary by company and can range from $400 to $2,000 per year, depending on which policy (and company) you choose.

There is a six-month open enrollment period for Medigap policies, during which time the insurance companies must insure everyone who is eligible for Medicare, regardless of medical history, health status, or claims experience. This six-month window starts when you enroll in Medicare Part B. So if you sign up for both Part A and Part B when you turn 65, you'll want to purchase Medigap insurance sometime during the following six months to take advantage of the open enrollment period. If you sign up for Part A only at age 65 because you are still covered by your employer's policy, your six-month period begins when your employer coverage stops and you sign up for Part B.

Medicare Managed Care Plans

Managed care plans are sometimes called coordinated care or prepaid plans or health maintenance organizations (HMOs). They might be thought of as a combination insurance company and doctor/hospital. Like an insurance company, they cover health care costs in return for a monthly premium, and like a doctor or hospital, they provide health care services. Each plan has its own network of hospitals, skilled nursing facilities, home health agencies, doctors, and other professionals. Depending on how the plan is organized, services are usually provided either at one or more centrally located health care facilities or in the private practice offices of the doctors who are part of the plan. Most managed care plans ask you to select a primary care doctor who will be responsible for managing your medical care, admitting you to a hospital, and referring you to specialists. In addition to paying the Part B premium to Medicare, you may also have to pay a fixed monthly premium to the plan and small copayments each time you go to the doctor or use other services. You do not pay Medicare's deductible and coinsurance. Usually there are no additional charges no matter how many times you visit the doctor, are hospitalized, or use other covered services. Some plans offer a point-of-service (POS) option, which allows you to receive certain services outside the plan's established provider network and the plan will pay a percentage of the charges. In return for this flexibility, you must pay a portion of the cost.

Medicare managed care plans are offered by private HMOs that have a contract with Medicare. You can find out which companies offer service in your area by contacting your local Social Security office. To enroll, you must have Part B and live in the plan's service area.

Non-Medicare Options

If you are not yet eligible for Medicare and will be losing your employer's health care coverage, you'll need to shop around for private insurance. You basically have a choice between the traditional fee-for-service plan and an HMO or managed care plan. With a fee-for-service plan, you pay monthly premiums to an insurance company. When you need medical care, you go to any doctor for treatment and then file a claim with the insurance company, who will either pay the doctor or reimburse you for your costs. With a managed care plan, you pay your premiums to the HMO. When you need medical care you go to that particular HMO. There are pros and cons to each type of plan. Generally, people who want to choose their own doctors opt for fee-for-service, while HMOs are appealing due to their comprehensive benefits and emphasis on prevention. Since you can usually get a better policy by being part of a group, check out various associations, like your college alumni association or any professional groups you may belong to.

Shopping for Health Insurance

When you retire, you will want to examine your health insurance options thoroughly and choose the type of coverage that works best for you and your family. As an employee, you were limited to what your employer offered. As a "free agent" you can explore many different kinds of health insurance, weigh the costs and coverages of each, and choose the plan that suits your needs. Before going shopping, examine your own health situation, including your medical history, your family history, your current lifestyle and any special medical needs you have. It's extremely important to choose the health plan that fits you personally, rather than opting for a program that may offer the broadest (and most expensive) coverage.

LONG-TERM CARE

Nowhere in Medicare's list of covered benefits will you see the words "long-term care." That's because Medicare does not cover long stays in nursing homes or custodial care facilities. With the cost of nursing home care averaging $50,000 a year, how do you protect against the possibility of you, your spouse or your parents needing to spend five, ten, fifteen years in a nursing home and draining your life savings to pay for it? Scary thought, isn't it? There are basically three ways you can deal with this dilemma.

STAY HEALTHY AND HOPE FOR THE BEST

Several studies have been done to determine the odds of people ending up in a nursing home sometime before they die. But all the studies show different results, so they're of little help in determining whether you have a nursing home in your future. Besides, you are not a statistic. Instead, look at your family history. Look at your health and lifestyle choices. And also consider your constitutional makeup and your determination to stay active and healthy in mind and body as you grow older. We don't mean to be Pollyannaish about this issue, but this may be one of those areas where you choose to accept the risk—while maintaining a positive attitude that it could never happen to you. When you start investigating long-term care insurance (see below), you may decide that ignoring the problem and hoping it will go away is the best solution after all.

DRAIN YOUR ASSETS AND GO ON MEDICAID

If you absolutely require long-term care and do not have the means to pay for it, the government will cover the cost through your state's Medicaid program. To become eligible for Medicaid you must spend down your savings and have no more than about $2,000 in assets. (In some states a spouse may keep up to $80,000 to prevent him or her from becoming destitute). There are strict rules about transferring assets to family members in order to qualify for Medicaid, so don't try this without guidance from an attorney. Clearly, this is not an attractive option: The assets are gone, the quality of care provided by Medicaid-approved facilities may be questionable, and then there's the humiliation of having to rely on the state welfare system. Maybe long-term care insurance is a wiser choice after all.

Buy Long-Term Care Insurance

Long-term care insurance is designed to cover some of the cost of a lengthy stay in a nursing home or care facility. These policies are relatively new, which makes some people nervous. Without a long claims history, how do the insurance companies know how to achieve that delicate balance between premiums flowing into the pot and payments flowing out? What makes most types of insurance work is that far fewer people file claims than pay premiums. But if you believe the insurance companies when they imply that practically everybody will end up in a nursing home before they die, how do the companies intend to make this whole thing work? Something to think about while we get on with the nuts and bolts of these policies.

Long-term care insurance pays for the cost of the day-in, day-out care for a person with an acute or long-term illness or disability. Care can range from personal care at home, including help with daily activities, to skilled nursing services in a nursing home. Coverage is generally triggered when a doctor certifies that the patient needs help performing two or more activities of daily living (ADLs), such as eating, bathing, dressing, moving from a bed to a chair, or getting to the toilet. After an *elimination period*, which lasts from 0 to 100 days, policies pay a fixed daily benefit—typically from $50 to $250 per day. Some policies offer inflation protection, either through automatic benefit increases or the right to buy additional insurance in the future (at whatever rates the company is charging at that time). As with all insurance, the more bells and whistles you opt for, the more it will cost you. Age is an important consideration with long-term care insurance. A policy that costs a 50-year-old $500 a year may cost a 65-year-old $2,000.

The biggest advantage to buying long-term care insurance is the obvious: It may prevent you from having to drain the family assets if you or a spouse or a parent ends up spending years in a nursing home at $100 or $150 a day. The biggest drawback is that you could run out of coverage, end up draining your assets, and have to go on Medicaid anyway—after paying thousands of dollars in premiums to the insurance company. Long-term care is an extremely important issue for anyone doing retirement planning, and it warrants far more information and discussion than we are able to provide here. We recommend that you open a family dialogue about it, gather information on long-term care policies (from the big, financially strong insurance companies only!), and give the matter serious consideration.

One compromise solution some families are using is to insure the younger, healthier spouse only, assuming that she (or he) can take care of the other. After all, the spouse who lives the longest is the one who really needs the insurance. Another idea is *self insurance*. Put the same amount of money you would normally pay out in long-term care insurance premiums into an investment account. If you never need the care, you can use the money for other purposes or pass it on to your heirs.

LIFE INSURANCE

As your need for good health insurance and possibly long-term care insurance increases during your retirement years, your need for life insurance decreases. It was when you were working and supplying the family with essential income that your death would have wreaked the most havoc. This is not to say that you won't be missed, but now that the kids have left the nest and you have little or no earned income to replace, what harm would there be if you died now? If you are paying premiums out of habit, or hanging onto your old whole-life policy because it just doesn't feel right not to carry life insurance, you may want to revisit some long-held notions about life insurance.

There are two main reasons to carry life insurance. One is to provide dependents with financial support if you should happen to make a hasty exit before your time. The other is to cover final expenses so your passing will not place a financial burden on the ones you leave behind. So think about who is depending on you for financial support and what would happen to them if you died. If the bulk of your income is generated by assets (investment account and IRAs) that will pass to your spouse upon your death, for example, that income will not be affected by your death so you don't need life insurance to replace it. It's quite possible that at this stage of your life no one is depending on you for support—your kids are grown, your spouse has his or her own income—which means you don't need to carry life insurance for its income replacement value.

You still may want to have life insurance to cover final expenses, however. It's up to you. The main expenses that you might possibly leave behind include: (1) final medical bills not covered by insurance, (2) burial expenses, (3) mortgages and other debts you want paid off, and (4) estate taxes and probate fees (if you have a large estate). Still, it's not mandatory that you have insurance to cover these items. If you have enough liquid assets in your estate to cover these expenses, insurance isn't necessary. Your heirs can simply pay the expenses out of the assets you leave behind. Some people with very large estates consisting of illiquid assets like real estate and closely held businesses buy life insurance to cover the estate taxes at death so their relatives won't have to dip into their own money or sell assets at distressed prices to cover the taxes. If this sounds like you, talk to your attorney about estate planning strategies to reduce estate taxes.

So if you don't need life insurance for income replacement, and you don't need life insurance for final expenses, what are you doing with that old whole-life insurance policy stashed away in the desk drawer? You may want to think about cashing it in and putting the money to work earning higher returns in your retirement bucket—or putting it toward a long-term care policy you thought you couldn't afford. After all, the whole purpose of insurance is to transfer risk, and the bigger risk at this stage of your life is not that your death will leave loved ones financially strapped but that your long life in an impaired state will do so.

DISABILITY INSURANCE

The same arguments against life insurance for retirees also apply to disability insurance. If the bulk of your income is derived from investments and not work, your income would not be in jeopardy if you were to become disabled. However, if you are between the ages of 50 and 65 and still working, you may want to think about disability insurance to replace your income should you become disabled and unable to work. After all, if you become disabled your own expenses must be covered, even if you have no nonworking family members depending on your income. To calculate how much disability insurance you need, first figure your monthly take-home pay after taxes. Next, call Social Security at 800-772-1213 and find out how much Social Security would pay if you were disabled. (Many cases of disability do not quality for Social Security benefits so you should probably not count on receiving them.) Next, ask your company benefits manager what kind of benefits you would receive if you were to become disabled. Now add up any other sources of income you may have, such as investment earnings, and subtract the total from your current monthly take-home pay. That's how much you need in disability benefits to maintain your current after-tax income.

If you decide to buy a disability insurance policy to supplement the benefits you already have, look for the following:

When do benefits begin? Most insurance companies give you a choice about how long you have to wait before benefits begin, anywhere from thirty days to a year. The longer you are willing to wait, the lower the premium. Check to see what resources would be available to you immediately following a disability and choose the longest waiting period you can reasonably handle.

How long should benefits last? It's probably wise to have benefits continue until you reach age 65 when Social Security starts.

How is disability defined? This is a tricky one, because disability can be defined in many different ways. Does it mean you can't do any work at all? Does it mean you can't do your regular work? "Own occupation" policies are more expensive, so you may have to plan on switching careers if you encounter a disability that prevents you from performing your regular job. But that may not be so bad. The main thing you're insuring against is loss of income in case you can't work at all.

HOMEOWNERS' INSURANCE

You wouldn't think of going without homeowners' insurance. Even though the odds of your house burning down or a major robbery occurring are, thankfully, very slim, the consequences of such disasters, if they were to occur, could devastate your family financially. In the case of homeowners' insurance, you are happy to pay into the big pot and hope never to take anything out. That's why you'll want to review your homeowners' insurance every so often to make sure it still meets your needs.

How much coverage do you need? Experts recommend that you base your insurance on replacement value rather than market value or the amount you paid for the house and its contents. After all, if disaster strikes you will need to rebuild and replace, so these other methods of valuation are meaningless. Insurance companies have guidelines based on square footage, building material, and other criteria, but you may want to do your own estimates after talking with contractors and factoring in any special features you may want in a replacement home, such as fancy moldings or custom hardwood floors. Remember that replacement value may have nothing to do with market value. Market value includes the house and the land. Replacement value just the house. Even so, the cost of building a new home could be substantially more than buying an existing home. Homeowners' policies used to include a provision guaranteeing "full replacement value" even if the replacement cost exceeded the amount of insurance carried. Recently, however, insurance companies have determined that this is not economically feasible and have shifted the onus of keeping property coverage up to date back to the policyholder.

Ideally, you should insure your home for 100 percent of its replacement value, but in any case no less than 80 percent. Insurance companies require that you carry at least 80 percent of replacement value in order to be fully reimbursed in the case of a partial loss. If you carry 80 percent and sustain a $10,000 loss, you will receive the entire $10,000; but if you carry only 60 percent, (three-quarters of the required 80 percent), you'll receive only $7,500, or three-quarters of the damage. Don't make the mistake of insuring up to the value of your mortgage. That would protect the mortgage holder but cause you to lose your entire equity in the home.

What about inflation? If your homeowners' policy does not have inflation protection and you haven't changed your policy in several years, this would be an excellent time to revisit your policy. Even at low levels of inflation, the cost of building a home can escalate before you know it. On the other hand, if your policy does have an automatic inflation adjustment, check to see that it hasn't boosted your coverage—and your premiums—higher than necessary.

What about that diamond brooch? If you've collected a lifetime of personal treasures like jewelry, antiques, artwork, and furniture, you will probably need extra coverage for these items. Most homeowners' policies cover only $1,000 or $2,000 for things like jewelry, stamp collections, and silverware. So take an inventory of what you have, get an independent appraisal of the more valuable items, and sit down with your insurance agent to see what you have to do to make sure these items are covered, whether it's adding a rider to your existing policy or taking out an additional policy. Once again, we'd like to suggest that you use your judgment when buying any kind of insurance. Sentimental value can never be replaced no matter how much insurance you carry.

What about liability? If a delivery man slips on your sidewalk and breaks his leg, your homeowners' policy should cover the costs associated with a lawsuit. Still, there may be certain limitations, so check with your insurance agent to see if you are adequately covered for mishaps that happen to other people while in your home. (And read the section on umbrella policies below.)

What about floods and earthquakes? Floods and earthquakes are horrible disasters that don't happen very often, but when they do, they leave their victims in total financial ruin. That's why most homeowners' policies don't cover them. If you want protection against floods or earthquakes, you must take out separate policies, which can be expensive. You can mitigate the cost somewhat by having a high deductible. Or you can go without and hope for the best. You decide.

Automobile insurance

Automobile insurance is another type of insurance that you can't afford to go without. But you can get the most for your money by being smart about your driving habits and policy selection. The thing that has the most dramatic impact on the cost of insurance is the value of your car. Drive an old clunker and you'll pay next to nothing in insurance. (Be sure to cancel the collision and comprehensive; they're not worth it on an old car.) High-profile cars and sports cars, on the other hand, are more expensive to insure because they're more attractive to thieves and tend to be involved in more accidents (even if *you've* never had an accident). Other ways to reduce your car insurance premiums are to raise your deductible from $250 to $500 and cancel any medical coverage that may be duplicated in your health insurance. Of course, you will ask about discounts, especially the ones that reward drivers who are over 55 and retired. Being a good driver and having multiple policies with the same insurer can save you money. And don't ignore the financial benefits of driving safely, taking defensive driving classes, using seat belts or airbags, and even having low mileage—some or all of these things can qualify you for additional discounts.

Umbrella policies and special insurance

If you have a nagging feeling that the traditional types of insurance discussed in this chapter do not fully protect you, consider taking out a personal liability (umbrella) policy to fill in the gaps. The more assets you have, the more important it is to protect them. Umbrella policies extend the coverage of your homeowners' and automobile policies, with a special focus on liability, an issue of great importance to wealthy individuals in a litigious society. Here are some things to think about:

Do you mix business with pleasure? If a neighbor slips on your sidewalk and injures herself, your homeowners' policy would cover it. But if a client slips on your sidewalk, your insurance company could say your policy doesn't cover business-related incidents. A personal umbrella policy usually doesn't cover business pursuits either, so depending on the extent of your business dealings, you may need a separate policy.

Do you own an attractive nuisance? An attractive nuisance is a sparkling swimming pool or other feature that could lure unsuspecting neighbors onto your property where they could get hurt. Do you own a snowmobile, motorbike, boat, airplane, or other dangerous vehicle? You'll need to have special insurance in case of mishaps.

Do you hire domestic help? Depending on the laws in your state, you may need to carry workers' compensation insurance for workers who come into your home. Some umbrella policies include worker's compensation, others don't. If yours doesn't, you'll have to take out a separate policy.

With all insurance, it is important to keep in mind that when a loss occurs, it is the claims adjuster who determines what will be covered under the policy, not the agent who sold it to you. Some insurance agents are very knowledgeable when it comes to helping you determine the kind and amount of insurance you need; others are salespeople who simply want to sell you the most coverage possible. Insurance in general is difficult to understand—the policies are written in legalese, and it's hard to find loopholes even though they're there. Do not let yourself be intimidated by the arcane nature of these documents. Ask questions until you fully understand what you're paying for— and what you can expect when you file a claim. The time to get this information is *before* you sign the policy, not after a disaster has already occurred.

CHAPTER FOURTEEN

Inflation

A nickel ain't worth a dime anymore.

—Yogi Berra

The hardest part about retirement planning is predicting the future. And since a big part of retirement planning is estimating your future expenses so you can make sure you have enough income to cover them, you're going to have to deal with this ominous thing called inflation. Now, normally, we discuss inflation in a very threatening way, warning you that if you're living on $40,000 a year now, and if inflation averages just 3 percent, you'll need $72,000 in twenty years just to stay even. And we talk about those poor retirees in the 1970s who were blindsided by a double-digit inflation rate that nobody could have predicted. And we tell you not to listen when Alan Greenspan cheers the low inflation rate and tells everybody not to worry, because your personal inflation rate is likely to be a lot higher due to medical bills and travel costs.

The reason we do this is because we do not want you to run out of money. We want to scare the bejeebers out of you so you'll invest your money wisely and earn a rate of return several points above the inflation rate. Then when the time comes for you to start taking income, we want you to drain your retirement bucket slowly and carefully, letting the remaining assets grow because you're going to need more income later on due to inflation.

The truth is that nobody can predict inflation. All you can do is prepare for it. You can buy insurance for practically any kind of disaster, but when it comes to the risk of running out of your life savings because your expenses outstripped your assets, no insurance company would touch that one with a ten-foot pole. So you have to assume the risk yourself—and put safeguards in place so it doesn't happen to you.

WHAT INFLATION IS

Inflation happens when prices go up. There are lots of forces influencing prices, but they pretty much boil down to two things. On one hand, prices may be "pulled" up by high demand at the consumer level—people want the product and are willing to pay a higher price to get it. On the other hand, prices may be "pushed" up by high costs at the producer level—increases in raw materials costs get passed on to the customer. If prices go up too high too fast (outstripping demand), people refuse to buy and stuff goes on sale. But if prices inch up little by little on items that people need and want, the price hikes hold and then people get used to paying more for everything.

The official measure of inflation is the Consumer Price Index (CPI), which keeps track of price changes of goods and services purchased for consumption by urban households. As shown in Table 14.1, this "market basket" of goods and services is grouped into eight major categories with the indicated relative weightings.

Altogether, there are some 90,000 items in the basket. Each item is specifically defined in order to make the index statistically accurate. For example, "apples" may be defined as "a 4.4-pound bag of golden delicious apples, U.S. extra fancy grade." To determine the relative importance of each category, the

TABLE 14.1   CONSUMER PRICE INDEX

EXPENDITURE CATEGORY	RELATIVE IMPORTANCE (%)
HOUSING (residential rent, homeowners' costs, furniture, fuel oil, soaps and detergents)	40
TRANSPORTATION (airline fares, new and used cars, gasoline, car insurance)	18
FOOD AND BEVERAGE (cookies, cereals, cheese, coffee, chicken, beer and ale, restaurant meals)	16
MEDICAL CARE (prescription drugs, eye care, physicians' services, hospital rooms)	6
RECREATION (cable TV, newspapers, toys, pet products, musical instruments, sports equipment, admissions)	6
APPAREL AND UPKEEP (men's shirts, women's dresses, jewelry)	5
EDUCATION AND COMMUNICATION (tuition, postage, telephone services, computers)	5
OTHER GOODS AND SERVICES (haircuts, cosmetics, bank fees, tobacco)	4

Bureau of Labor Statistics (BLS) obtains spending information from about 29,000 individuals and families in eighty-seven urban areas throughout the country. BLS representatives then call or visit some 23,000 businesses, including retail stores, service establishments, rental units, and doctors' offices all over the United States to obtain price information. Since it takes a while to compile all this information, the index lags the actual dates on which prices were obtained. The 1999 CPI reflects prices from 1994, 1995, and 1996.

The CPI was first developed during World War I to enable the federal government to establish cost-of-living adjustments for workers in shipbuilding centers due to the rapid price increases taking place at that time. Regular publication of a national index began in 1921, starting with 145 selected items in thirty-two industrial cities. Since that time, the CPI has been updated five times.

Just recently, the BLS made a major change in the way the index is calculated. Responding to complaints that the CPI did not reflect people's actual buying patterns—that when the price of iceberg lettuce is too high people switch to romaine, or when their neighborhood hardware store gets too expensive they go to The Home Depot—it changed the way the index is calculated to reflect these substitutions. Before, it assumed people blindly paid whatever price was charged. Now, it takes into account the fact that people have become smart shoppers. The effect has been to reduce the inflation rate a few tenths of a percentage point.

Table 14.2 shows what the inflation rate has been in the past.

HOW INFLATION AFFECTS YOU

There are a number of ways inflation affects you, and they're not all bad. Starting with the CPI and how it's used by the federal government to set policies, let's look at some of the more common instances where you are affected by "inflation adjustments."

SOCIAL SECURITY

The biggest area affecting retirees is the cost-of-living adjustment (COLA), which raises your Social Security check every year. When calculating the COLA, the Social Security Administration uses the CPI for the one-year period ending in September to determine how much higher benefits will be for the following year. The COLA announced in late 1998 for benefits starting in January 1999 was the lowest in history (tying the rate

TABLE **14.2**   CONSUMER PRICE INDEX,
ANNUAL % CHANGE

YEAR	% CHANGE	YEAR	% CHANGE	YEAR	% CHANGE
1914	1.0	1942	9.0	1970	5.6
1915	2.0	1943	3.0	1971	3.3
1916	12.6	1944	2.3	1972	3.4
1917	18.1	1945	2.2	1973	8.7
1918	20.4	1946	18.1	1974	12.3
1919	14.5	1947	8.8	1975	6.9
1920	2.6	1948	3.0	1976	4.9
1921	−10.8	1949	−2.1	1977	6.7
1922	−2.3	1950	5.9	1978	9.0
1923	2.4	1951	6.0	1979	13.3
1924	0.0	1952	0.8	1980	12.5
1925	3.5	1953	0.7	1981	8.9
1926	−1.1	1954	−0.7	1982	3.8
1927	−2.3	1955	0.4	1983	3.8
1928	−1.2	1956	3.0	1984	3.9
1929	0.6	1957	2.9	1985	3.8
1930	-6.4	1958	1.8	1986	1.1
1931	-9.3	1959	1.7	1987	4.4
1932	−10.3	1960	1.4	1988	4.4
1933	0.8	1961	0.7	1989	4.6
1934	1.5	1962	1.3	1990	6.1
1935	3.0	1963	1.6	1991	3.1
1936	1.4	1964	1.0	1992	2.9
1937	2.9	1965	1.9	1993	2.7
1938	−2.8	1966	3.5	1994	2.7
1939	0.0	1967	3.0	1995	2.5
1940	0.7	1968	4.7	1996	3.3
1941	9.9	1969	6.2		

in 1986)—1.3 percent. Retirees weren't quite sure how to react to this news. While they were understandably upset that their checks would not be going up by much, on the other hand, it's hard to curse a low inflation rate.

INCOME TAX

You'll recall from our discussion on taxes that both the personal exemption and the standard deduction are indexed to inflation. This means that when the CPI rises, you get more tax deductions. This effectively reduces your tax bill, all other things being equal.

RETIREMENT PLAN CONTRIBUTIONS

If you are still working and contributing to a 401(k) plan, your maximum contribution is indexed to inflation. So when the CPI goes up, you get to shelter more of your income from taxes by contributing more to your retirement plan. Because inflation has been so low in recent years, the maximum contribution did not change from 1998 to 1999; it remained stable at $10,000.

SALARY AND WAGES

If you work for a company that grants automatic cost-of-living salary increases, your income goes up with inflation. Of course, this may offset those higher tax deductions mentioned earlier, but the idea behind cost-of-living adjustments is not to make people better off but rather to keep them from falling behind.

AT THE CHECKOUT COUNTER

As a consumer, inflation affects the prices you pay for things. You may not notice small price increases here and there, but they do catch up with you over time. Now, if your income is keeping pace with inflation, you can manage these price increases just fine. But if you are living on a fixed income, inflation can be a real problem. And that's why we want you to arrange your finances during retirement so your income will *not* be fixed. We want you to have enough assets in reserve—and to keep those assets growing all the time—to allow your income to go up along with inflation. Once again we want to emphasize that you must take care of this yourself. Social Security cost-of-living adjustments go only so far. If the majority of your income comes from other sources, you'll need to build in your own cost-of-living adjustments.

One of the complaints Social Security recipients had when the 1.3 percent COLA was announced in 1998 was that the CPI does not reflect *their* spending habits. Medical care, for example, represents just 6 percent of the index, but many seniors spend a far greater percentage of their income on medical care. With the cost of medical care outstripping the general inflation rate—it has ranged from 3 to 10 percent in recent years—some seniors are indeed falling behind. This has led some to question whether the general Consumer Price Index should be used for Social Security COLAs or whether a special index should be created that better reflects the buying habits of Social Security recipients.

WHAT YOU CAN DO ABOUT INFLATION

Now that you understand what the Consumer Price Index is and how it's created, we'd like to suggest that you design your own Personal Price Index (PPI—not to be confused with the government's Producer Price Index) so you can keep track of your own inflation rate. If there's one lesson we have all learned from the past, it's that inflation can be insidious. It creeps up on you if you don't watch out. A few pennies extra at the grocery store every week adds up to dollars over time without your even being aware of it. Then one day you look up and realize that a box of cereal—which used to be 16 ounces but is now 12—costs $4.00. You remember when cereal cost 89 cents. When did it get to be *four dollars?*

KEEP TRACK OF PRICES

The first thing you can do is start a notebook that lists the prices you are accustomed to paying for things. On a typical shopping trip, write down the price of bread, milk, toilet paper, and the like. Depending on how carried away you want to get with this, you can log everything you buy, or you can select a representative sampling. Do this not just for the grocery store but for other things you buy, such as electricity, car insurance, meals out, prescription drugs, and so on. There are two reasons for keeping track of prices this way. One is so you can be a smart comparison shopper. If you normally pay $2.39 for a loaf of bread and you see it on sale for $1.99, you'll know it's a bargain and you might want to buy several loaves and freeze them. The other reason is so you can track price increases over time. When bread goes up to $2.49 then $2.59, your notebook will show you that you're paying more. Otherwise you may not notice.

DESIGN YOUR OWN PERSONAL PRICE INDEX

The next thing you can do is design your own Personal Price Index. This will take some time to set up, but it'll be worth it in the long run. If you consider it a game, it actually can be fun. Over the next twelve months, keep track of all of your expenditures, including credit card charges, checks you write, and cash you spend, and categorize them similar to the CPI categories listed in Table 14.1. (You can use different categories if you want, and you can add subcategories to track your spending better; a software program like Quicken will help you do this easily.) At the end of the first year, add up your total expenditures as well as the total for each category. This will be your baseline index. Every year thereafter, keep track of your spending in a similar manner and compare the totals to the previous year. Note the percentage change for the total as well as for each category. Just as the government uses the CPI to make adjustments in its various programs, you can use your own PPI to make adjustments in your own spending and investing programs. Depending on the results, you can either cut back on spending or beef up the income side of the equation, by investing more aggressively or considering other income opportunities. The whole point of this exercise is to keep you aware of the balance between your expenses and your income year by year and not to let so much time go by that it becomes too late to do anything about it.

BE FLEXIBLE

Inflation can really hurt when it hits the things you must have and there are no alternatives, like some prescription drugs. However, there's a lot you *can* do about inflation if you become aware of it early enough and are willing to be flexible in your buying habits. Table 14.3 presents some ideas for coping with inflation. You'll be able to think of more on your own.

TABLE 14.3   IDEAS FOR COPING WITH INFLATION

IF THIS HAPPENS . . .	TRY THIS
HOUSING	
Your electricity bill goes up	Adopt standard conservation measures like turning down the thermostat, taking short showers, and using energy-efficient appliances
Your property tax bill goes up	Challenge the appraisal
The plumber wants to charge $300 to fix a couple of leaky faucets	Do it yourself
Your homeowners' insurance goes up	Reduce coverage or raise the deductible; shop for a new insurance carrier
Your rent gets raised	Move
Your phone bill goes up	Cancel services you're not using; switch to another long-distance carrier
FOOD	
Your grocery bills are getting higher	Buy in bulk at discount warehouses and shop at your neighborhood store for specialty items only; stick to a list and use coupons

If This Happens . . .	Try This
You're spending more on meals out	Go out for the entree only; have drinks and dessert at home
The price of your favorite wine goes up	Find another favorite
TRANSPORTATION	
Your car insurance goes up	Reduce coverage, raise the deductible, shop around for another carrier; ask for discounts
You're spending a lot on gasoline	Buy the lowest-octane gas and pump it yourself; drive less
You're spending a lot on repairs and maintenance	Change the oil yourself; learn how to do simple repairs like changing spark plugs; find a good, honest mechanic
MEDICAL AND DENTAL	
You're spending a lot on prescription drugs	Buy the generic brand; consider alternative medicine
Your health insurance premiums are going up	Shop for a new policy/carrier
Your doctor bills are too high	Adopt healthy habits and treat yourself at home whenever possible
CLOTHING AND PERSONAL ITEMS	
You're spending too much on clothes	Don't be a slave to fashion; keep your wardrobe simple
You're spending too much at the hair salon	Color your hair yourself; go longer between haircuts
Dry-cleaning bills are going up	Don't buy anything that has to be dry cleaned

(continued on next page)

If This Happens . . .	Try This
RECREATION/TRAVEL/EDUCATION	
Airline tickets are going up	Take advantage of discounts such as Saturday stays and advance purchases; consider flying out of alternative airports; keep an eye out for fare wars
You spend too much on books	Use the library
Your hobbies are too expensive	Find new hobbies

The purpose of this table is to show that there are many, many ways you can reduce your expenditures if you have to. We are not trying to turn you into a penny-pincher but to show you that if inflation does start to rob you of purchasing power, there's nearly always some fat you can cut out of your budget, as long as you stay flexible in your buying habits. In the meantime, keep that retirement bucket growing so you'll have plenty of reserves to draw from.

Arranging
Your Affairs

CHAPTER FIFTEEN

Health Care and Daily Living

One of the most difficult things to contend with in a
hospital is the assumption on the part of the staff
that because you have lost your gall bladder
you have also lost your mind.

—Jean Kerr

You think it will never happen to you. You *hope* it will never happen to you. But if it does, you may not even know it. What are we talking about? The possibility that you might someday be incapable of taking care of yourself. The incapacity could range from forgetting to pay a utility bill to the inability to communicate with your doctor about important health care decisions. We've all heard horror stories about elderly people suffering physical or mental declines and doing irreparable physical or financial harm to themselves before caring family members find out about it and step in to help. Don't let this happen to you.

We're all for maintaining a positive attitude throughout life. But a big part of retirement planning is contemplating the worst so you can prepare for it and put it behind you. Once the arrangements are made, you can get on with your life and focus on the positive because the negative, should it occur, has already been taken care of. To be set for life is not just having enough money to last the rest of your life but also having your affairs arranged the way you want them, so you'll know that if you were to become incapacitated—whether by an automobile accident tomorrow or a stroke at age 95—your wishes will be carried out. The ultimate goal of all this retirement planning business is peace of mind. But peace of mind will forever elude you until you've taken care of the final details.

Note to readers with aging parents: Throughout this book we are discussing the various retirement planning strategies from the perspective of the retiree, or older individual. But if you are responsible for aging parents, please read this and the next two chapters with your parents in mind. The next chapter on disposition of assets can be a touchy subject for parents and children to discuss, but this chapter on assisted living and advance directives is something you'll all want to talk about. Not only will it give your parents an opportunity to tell you how they want to be cared for in their old age, it may open up a dialogue on how they want their assets distributed so you can help them with wills and trusts as discussed in the next chapter.

ALTERNATIVE LIVING ARRANGEMENTS—WHEN LIVING AT HOME ISN'T WORKING ANYMORE

As you grow older, you may find that fully independent living isn't working anymore. Maybe you've just lost a spouse who had been helping you around the house. Maybe a fall or accident has left you unable to get around as easily as you used to. Maybe you're just lonely and would like to have more daily contact with other people. Even if none of these situations applies to you now, it's never too soon to explore alternative living arrangements, because you never know when you will need them. The living arrangements listed below all have certain features that you'll want to evaluate and match to your own needs. Because this evaluation can be a lengthy process—studying the various features, finding suitable facilities, visiting them and talking with staff, evaluating the financial arrangements, having your lawyer review the contracts—you'll want to start long before the need becomes urgent. Besides, some of the better facilities have waiting lists, so you may not be able to get in right away.

Twenty years ago, there weren't many options for people who found themselves unable to live independently at home. They either moved into a nursing home or perhaps stayed with relatives. For most families, neither option was ideal. Nursing homes, many of which reeked of sickness and old age, were inappropriate for people who just wanted a small amount of help with daily living activities. Staying with relatives, both then and now, can place an undue burden on the primary caregiver, who often has young children to care for as well. Even the healthiest of families have cracked under the strain of caring for an aging relative or at least suffered guilt and anxiety when they chose not to do so.

Fortunately, there are many options available for assisted living today. Some even offer varying levels of service to allow you to stay in the same facility as your need for care increases.

INDEPENDENT LIVING FACILITIES

For active, healthy retirees who want to replace the responsibilities of home maintenance with the joy of recreational activities, independent living facilities are one step removed from fully independent living. They are similar to any apartment, condominium, or single-family development, except that they provide special services, including security and a full range of activities that promote social contact among residents. Shopping trips, outings to cultural events, and organized gatherings are typical activities. Many independent living communities also have tennis courts, swimming pools, activity rooms, and other amenities. Most offer a variety of meal plans, including the option of preparing meals in your own apartment. Some independent living communities are affiliated with health care facilities that can provide such care when it is needed. You also can purchase home health care services from outside providers. Most independent living communities are rental communities, but a few are condominiums or single-family developments in which you own your own unit or home. Costs and services vary widely. In some communities a monthly fee covers many services, while in others a fee-for-service system is used.

CONTINUING CARE RETIREMENT COMMUNITIES (CCRCs)

CCRCs embrace the concept of "life-care," an idea that evolved from the realization that people don't want to move from place to place seeking different levels of care. You start out in a private apartment, where you function independently. Then as your need for assistance increases, you can move to an assisted living suite and then to a private room in the CCRC's nursing care wing. There are generally three basic types of contracts: extensive, modified, and fee-for-service. An *extensive contract* covers shelter, residential services, and amenities, plus unlimited long-term nursing care without an increase in monthly payments (except for normal increases related to operating costs and inflation adjustments). Entrance fees and monthly costs under extensive contracts are typically higher than those under modified or fee-for-service contracts. A *modified contract* covers shelter, residential services, and amenities, plus a specified amount of nursing care. After the specified amount of care has been received, you can continue to receive care on an unlimited basis, but you must pay for it at daily or monthly nursing care rates. A *fee-for-service contract* covers shelter, residential services, and amenities. While emergency and short-term nursing care is usually included in the contract, access to long-term nursing care is guaranteed only at daily nursing care rates. Entrance and monthly fees are lower under this type of contract because you are responsible for all long-term nursing and health care costs.

Unfortunately, these communities aren't cheap. The more luxurious ones charge entrance fees of $300,000 or more and monthly fees of $4,000 or higher. Less-plush facilities charge an average entrance fee of $100,000 and monthly fees of $1,500. Because this is such a long-term commitment, it would be a good idea to have an attorney review the contract before you sign. Whatever fee arrangement you end up with, you'll want to make sure you'll be able to pay the fees for the remainder of your life, whether through personal assets, insurance, or a combination of the two.

ASSISTED LIVING FACILITIES

Assisted living facilities are designed for individuals who cannot function in an independent living environment but do not need nursing care on a daily basis. At an assisted living facility you can get help with bathing, dressing, meals, and housekeeping at a level that suits your needs. These communities go by a variety of names, including adult homes, personal care homes, retirement residences, and sheltered housing. They are often affiliated with independent living communities or nursing care facilities in order to offer a continuum of care for changing needs. Many assisted living facilities also have professional nurses and other health care professionals on staff or available on call in case you require special care. Most assisted living communities charge a monthly rent. In some cases, the fee covers only a few basic services, while in others it is all-inclusive, covering a multitude of services.

SKILLED NURSING HOMES

Nursing homes are for people who require nursing care on a regular basis but do not need to be hospitalized. The care is administered by nursing professionals under the direction of a physician, and the homes are regulated by state and local boards of health. Because this kind of care can be so expensive and be needed for so long, many people buy long-term care insurance (as discussed in Chapter 13) to help pay for it.

OTHER HOUSING OPTIONS

Here are some other options, in case community living is not for you.

Home Modifications
There are all kinds of things you can do to your house to make it easier to get around in, from bars in the bathroom, to wider

doorways, to ramps—even elevators—to help you go up and down stairs. Talk to a contractor who specializes in home modifications for people with disabilities.

Home Care

With someone to come in and help with daily living activities, or even skilled nursing services, you can remain in your home and get the care you need. Health aides, who help with bathing and shop for groceries, cost $10 to $18 per hour, while registered nurses, who perform more skilled services such as inserting catheters, cost $25 to $40 per hour.

Adult Day Care

Adult day-care centers can handle elders suffering from a variety of infirmities—including Alzheimer's disease—as long as the person is mobile and not disruptive to the group. Most adult centers provide breakfast and lunch as well as scheduled activities, such as music, exercise programs, and trips to the park. Most centers are open from 9:00 A.M. to 5:00 P.M. five days a week, and some offer transportation to and from the facility. Daily rates range from $30 for basic care to $150 for rehabilitation therapy and skilled nursing.

Home Sharing

In a home-sharing arrangement, you rent rooms to tenants—preferably younger people—who would help around the house. You would provide free rent in exchange for a certain number of hours of household chores.

Adult Foster Care

Adult foster care is another alternative. With foster care, you would live in a licensed provider's home and receive twenty-four-hour supervision, meals, laundry service, transportation, and personal care. Many of the providers have been trained by registered nurses or are themselves RNs. Typically, you'd get a private bedroom and use of the common rooms in the house. The cost ranges from $1,200 to $2,000 per month.

ADVANCE DIRECTIVES ALLOW YOU TO STATE YOUR WISHES BEFORE THE TIME COMES

An advance directive allows you to state your wishes before the time these wishes would be called into play. An advance directive can be as simple and informal as telling your doctor to avoid heroic measures if it means living out your days in a vegetative state. Or you can draft a formal document with very specific instructions. The important thing to remember about advance directives is that they can be changed at any time. If you're afraid of setting forth your wishes because you might change your mind about some things later, don't worry. It's better to get something down in writing; otherwise your loved ones will have no idea what you want.

LIVING WILL

A living will states the kind of medical care you want (or do not want) if you become unable to make your own decisions. It is called a living will because it takes effect while you are still living. Many states have their own living will forms, but you can draw up your own form or simply write a statement of your preferences for treatment. Although it is not mandatory, you may want to speak to an attorney or your physician to be sure you have completed the living will in a way that ensures your wishes will be understood and followed. The drawback to a living will is that it is very limited, usually covering only a small number of conditions and treatments. It also is a "static" document, which means your written instructions must stand on their own; no one is identified to interpret your wishes. A more powerful document for most people is the health care power of attorney, or health care proxy.

HEALTH CARE POWER OF ATTORNEY

With a health care power of attorney or health care proxy, you appoint another person, such as a spouse, grown child, or close friend, as your authorized spokesperson to make medical decisions for you if you should become unable to make them for yourself. You can also include instructions about any treatment you want to avoid. The difference between a health care power of attorney and a living will is that the person you appoint in the health care power of attorney is free to exercise his or her own judgment at the time a decision is called for. He or she can consult with the doctor, fully understand the ramifications of all possible decisions, and apply the knowledge of what you would want done when rendering what could be a life-or-death decision.

You do not have to be sick to draft a health care power of attorney. You also do not need to see an attorney or file the document with the court. If you wish to cancel an advance directive while you are in the hospital, all you need do is notify your doctor and your family. Even without a change in writing, your wishes stated in person directly to your doctor generally carry more weight than a living will or health care power of attorney—as long as you can decide for yourself and can communicate your wishes. But be sure to state your wishes clearly and be sure that they are understood.

Some people feel very strongly about the right to die naturally and with dignity. They may specify such things as no blood transfusions, no artificial feeding or breathing mechanisms, no antibiotics in the case of pneumonia or other serious infection, and no surgery if it looks like their condition is terminal. Other people, especially when they are healthy and haven't even contemplated serious illness yet, aren't prepared to be quite so specific. In this case, it's better to sign a health care power of attorney appointing a loved one to be in charge, make your general wishes known to your doctor and your loved one, and let that person make the final decisions if and when the time comes.

Because none of us knows when we might get hit by a truck, it's a good idea for everyone, regardless of age, to have a health care power of attorney naming a responsible loved one to make decisions on our behalf. If you haven't thought about such matters before, this may require some soul searching, followed by a frank discussion with the person you name as your health care agent. Once you have signed an advance directive, give a copy to your health care agent and ask your physician to make it a part of your permanent medical record. Keep a copy of it in a safe place, and carry a card in your wallet telling where your advance directive is located and how to contact your health care agent.

FUNERAL ARRANGEMENTS

Now, we know you're not anywhere near ready to die, but wouldn't it be a great relief to your loved ones to have all of your funeral wishes spelled out in advance so in their time of grief they won't have to make emotionally wrenching decisions—and risk getting ripped off by greedy funeral directors? You actually can go so far as to buy what are euphemistically called "pre-need" burial policies, prepaying your funeral expenses so your loved ones won't have to. These policies lock in today's prices, so they may be financially sound as well. But do shop around and also consider that you may be able to invest the money more wisely yourself.

But whether you prepay for your funeral or not, you can still specify your wishes in advance. Here are some issues to think about:

- Do you want to be buried or cremated?
- If buried, what kind of casket do you want?
- Do you want a formal service open to the public or an informal gathering of friends?
- Where will the service be conducted, in a church, synagogue, at graveside, or in a mortuary or cemetery chapel?
- Who will conduct the service?
- What music will be played?
- Do you want donations in lieu of flowers made to a favorite charity?

According to a price survey conducted by the National Funeral Directors Association in 1997, the typical American adult funeral cost $4,783. Cemetery expenses such as a grave site, interment, and marker can bring the total to $8,000 or so. You do not need to spend this much. There are a great many extra fees tacked onto funeral costs that loved ones, in their grieving state, are likely to pay without question. But by dispassionately arranging your own funeral—by picking out your own casket (and avoiding the super-deluxe $10,000 model) and wisely eschewing options that funeral directors will try to sell you—you can spare your loved ones much pain and many dollars.

CHAPTER SIXTEEN

Distribution of Assets

We make a living by what we get,
we make a life by what we give.

—Winston Churchill

There are three truths in this world about what you have when it's time to go. One, you can't take it with you. Two, if you don't specify where you want it to go, the state will decide for you. And three, if your estate exceeds the exemption equivalent—$650,000 in 1999 and rising to $1 million in 2006—your heirs (except your spouse) will have to pay taxes on the amount they inherit. It is these three truths that have spawned a huge estate planning industry and led to the creation of all kinds of fancy trusts designed to minimize the effects of the three truths—especially the third one. Do you need to know about all these fancy trusts? That depends on how big your estate is. The more assets you have at death, the more tax will be due, because our estate tax system is *progressive,* meaning it imposes a higher percentage of tax on higher levels of assets.

So before getting into all this estate planning business, you need to take a realistic look at what you have—and what you may be expected to have accumulated by the time you die—to see how far you need to go with tax-saving strategies. Keep in mind that by the time you add up your IRA rollover accounts, other investment accounts, and the value of your house, you can get up there pretty fast. And if you're being careful not to drain your retirement bucket too quickly—indeed, if your bucket is growing faster than the rate at which you're taking money out—you could have substantial assets by the time you die. You'll want to make sure Uncle Sam doesn't snatch too much of your hard-earned wealth and deprive your loved ones of the fruits of your labors.

So as you approach the end of your life, you'll need to make a shift in mind-set, from *accumulating* assets to *distributing* assets. Assets that are not part of your estate are not taxed, so the more you can get rid of before you die, the less tax your heirs will have to pay. All of this is very tricky, of course, because you don't want to get rid of so much that you don't have enough left for yourself. That's why smart attorneys have thought up all these fancy estate planning strategies designed to let you keep your assets and get rid of them at the same time.

How estate taxes are calculated

Estate tax is similar to income tax in that you start with your *gross estate* (everything you own minus everything you owe), subtract certain expenses to arrive at your *taxable estate*, refer to the estate tax schedule to determine the amount of *tax due*, and then subtract the *unified credit*, to arrive at your *net estate taxes*.

So let's say your taxable estate is worth $800,000. Referring to the estate tax rate schedule in Table 16.1, you see that your estate tax liability would be $248,300 (the amount of tax on $750,000) plus $19,500 (39 percent of the amount over $750,000, or $50,000), for a total of $267,800. When you subtract the unified credit of $211,300 for 1999 (see Table 16.2), you (or rather, your heirs) are left with an estate tax bill of $56,500. (Please note that this schedule applies to federal estate taxes only; state and local taxes are not considered here.)

TABLE **16.1** **ESTATE TAX SCHEDULE**

IF THE VALUE OF YOUR TAXABLE ESTATE IS BETWEEN:	AND:	YOUR TENTATIVE TAX IS	PLUS:	ON AMOUNTS OVER:
$ 0	$ 10,000	$ 0	18%	$ 0
10,000	20,000	1,800	20%	10,000
20,000	40,000	3,800	22%	20,000
40,000	60,000	8,200	24%	40,000
60,000	80,000	13,000	26%	60,000
80,000	100,000	18,200	28%	80,000
100,000	150,000	23,800	30%	10,000
150,000	250,000	38,000	32%	150,000
250,000	500,000	70,800	34%	250,000
500,000	750,000	155,800	37%	500,000
750,000	1,000,000	248,300	39%	750,000
1,000,000	1,250,000	345,800	41%	1,000,000
1,250,000	1,500,000	448,300	43%	1,250,000
1,500,000	2,000,000	555,800	45%	1,500,000
2,000,000	2,500,000	780,800	49%	2,000,000
2,500,000	3,000,000	1,025,800	53%	2,500,000
Over 3,000,000	—	1,290,800	55%	3,000,000

UNIFIED CREDIT AND EXEMPTION EQUIVALENT

The unified credit is an automatic tax credit that is applied to both lifetime gifts and assets transferred at death. (That's why it's called "unified.") Thanks to the unified credit, estates under $650,000 in 1999 pay no estate taxes at all. The *exemption equivalent*, or the highest value your estate can be to have the estate tax reduced to zero by the unified credit, is $650,000. The exemption equivalent and unified credit will be going up in future years as indicated in Table 16.2.

TABLE 16.2 INCREASE IN EXEMPTION EQUIVALENT AND UNIFIED CREDIT

YEAR	EXEMPTION EQUIVALENT	UNIFIED CREDIT
1999	$ 650,000	$211,300
2000	675,000	220,550
2001	675,000	220,550
2002	700,000	229,800
2003	700,000	229,800
2004	850,000	287,300
2005	950,000	326,300
2006	1,000,000	345,800

UNLIMITED MARITAL DEDUCTION

If you want all of your assets to go to your spouse, there is no estate tax due at the time of your death. This is called the *unlimited marital deduction*. It's when your spouse dies that the tax man will have his hand out. Assuming your spouse didn't spend everything you left him or her, that's when the total of what's left of your estate plus all of your spouse's estate would be taxed. One of the most basic estate planning strategies is to make sure both husband and wife fully utilize their respective unified credits so they can take advantage of the $1.3 million available to both of them ($650,000 × 2) that can pass tax free. In the $800,000 example above, if, instead of passing it all to your spouse, you were to give the first $650,000 to someone else (usually a trust, discussed below), only $150,000 would pass to your spouse. Then there would be no estate tax due at all, either at your death or your spouse's. The first $650,000 utilizes your unified credit, while your spouse's $150,000 is well under his or her $650,000 exemption equivalent amount, resulting in no tax.

WHAT IS PROBATE?

Probate is a court procedure that makes sure your assets go where you want them to go after you're gone. The probate process begins when your will is filed with the local probate court by your attorney or your *executor,* who is the person named in the will as the person with administrative responsibility to settle your estate's affairs. If no executor is named in your will, or if you die *intestate* (without a will), the court will appoint an *administrator,* who will handle such functions for a fee. During probate, the court will make sure that the will is valid—that it is not forged and that its provisions are legal. The court will then oversee the distribution of assets and final settlement of the estate. While there is no legal requirement to use an estate attorney, most people do, both to speed up the process and to ensure that they comply with all relevant state laws. Attorney fees are generally paid out of the estate and usually amount to 2 to 3 percent of the total value of the estate. Other probate costs include filing fees, accounting fees, appraisal fees, and any other costs that may be required to protect and distribute the assets. Because probate involves filing an inventory of the assets and liabilities of the deceased, these filings are generally open for public inspection. This is an issue of concern for some people.

The main advantage of probate is that it protects the beneficiaries and ensures that your wishes will be carried out. The main disadvantage of probate is that it is time-consuming, expensive, and public. To avoid probate, many people employ one or more of the estate planning strategies discussed in the next section.

HOW PROPERTY PASSES TO HEIRS

There are several ways you can pass property to your heirs:

- By gift
- By contract
- By operation of law
- By will
- By trust
- By your state's laws of succession

BY GIFT

By giving property away during your lifetime, you can make darn sure that the person you want to get it gets it. And, of course, lifetime gifts escape the probate process because probate is not triggered until after death. Large gifts do not escape taxes—otherwise people would give away everything on their deathbed and nobody would ever pay estate taxes. Instead, large gifts are added to your taxable estate to determine your "gift and estate tax" bill, from which the unified credit is subtracted, as discussed earlier. In other words, if you make a $50,000 gift during your lifetime, the amount of assets you can give away at death is reduced to $600,000. You can, however, give away $10,000 a year to as many people as you wish—your spouse can do the same for a total of $20,000 a year—without any gift or estate tax liability. Annual $10,000 gift-giving is a popular estate planning strategy among wealthy people who know their kids are going to get it all someday anyway.

One thing to remember when giving away appreciated property is that if you give it away during your lifetime, the person you give it to will inherit your cost basis as well. This means

he or she eventually will have to pay the income tax you're trying to avoid by giving it away. On the other hand, if you pass it
to people through inheritance, their cost basis is the value of
the asset at your death. For example, let's say you have 1,000
shares of a $10.00 stock that you bought for $1.00. If you give it
to your daughter during your lifetime, eventually she will have
to pay tax on all the appreciation over $1.00 ($9,000 if she sells
it right away). But if she receives it by inheritance, she'll pay tax
only on the appreciation over $10.00 (zero, if she sells it imme-
diately after inheriting it).

Also remember that in order to be a true gift, you must
relinquish all rights to it. You can't give away shares of stock but
continue to receive the dividends, for example, and you can't
give assets to a child but remain custodian of the account. If you
do, the assets will still be included in your estate.

By Contract

When you fill out a beneficiary designation form for your IRA
or pension plan, you are signing a contract that states who
should receive the property at your death. Annuity contracts
and life insurance contracts do the same thing. Be sure to check
the terms of each contract periodically to make sure that each
accurately reflects your intentions because property passes to
beneficiaries outside the will and probate process. In other
words, your ex-spouse could get your IRA even if your will says
you want everything to go to your new spouse.

You'll remember from Chapter 9 on individual retirement
accounts that your beneficiary designation can also affect your
minimum mandatory IRA withdrawals at age 70½. This is one
instance where your estate planning goal (leave everything to
your spouse) may conflict with your income tax planning goal
(minimize distributions by choosing a younger beneficiary, like
a grandchild). All you can do is be aware of the consequences of
the various choices and make the best decision you can. When
it comes to corporate pension plans, you must name your
spouse as beneficiary unless he or she signs a waiver giving up
his or her rights to the assets.

BY OPERATION OF LAW

When you hold property in joint tenancy with another person, your share automatically goes to the other person when you die, regardless of what is stated in your will. If you live in a community property state (Arizona, California, Idaho, Louisiana, Nevada, New Mexico, Texas, Washington, or Wisconsin), additional rules may apply. Property passing to a joint tenant does so outside the probate process. This is one reason many people like to hold their homes and brokerage accounts in joint names. But one common misconception people have is that property held in joint tenancy escapes estate and gift taxes as well. This is true for spouses due to the unlimited marital deduction, but not for other beneficiaries. The minute you add your daughter's name to your $100,000 brokerage account, you have just given her a taxable gift of $50,000.

BY WILL

A will is a written document that allows you to specify who should get what when you die. Although it's possible to draft a handwritten, or *holographic*, will, it's better to have an attorney draft your will to make sure it stands up in court. In addition to designating who should get your property after your death, you may also use a will to name a guardian for minor children. Also, in your will you should name the person you want to serve as executor of your estate. Most people name a family member, trusted friend, or advisor (accountant or attorney) to be executor. If you do not name an executor, a court-appointed administrator will perform the same duties for a fee.

BY TRUST

A trust is a legal device that allows you to transfer property to a trustee who will manage the assets for the benefit of the person you designate. A trust is one of those fancy ways to get property out of your estate without leaving yourself destitute. (More on trusts below.)

By the Laws of Succession in Your State

If you die without having in force any of the mechanisms just discussed, your state will decide where your property should go after your death. Now, it's quite possible that your state's laws are what you would want anyway, because the laws of succession generally follow accepted patterns of familial relationships (spouse first, kids next, parents after that, and so on). But the laws vary from state to state with regard to percentages—in some states the spouse gets everything, in others the spouse and kids share one-third/two-thirds, for example—so the safest thing to do is to state your wishes using a will or some other legal device.

Popular estate planning strategies

Estate planning is a huge industry consisting of mostly honest and some not-so-honest attorneys and life insurance representatives. Most people, when first introduced to the various loopholes that allow them to save estate taxes and get around other parts of the law such as probate, are naturally skeptical. "Is this really legal?" they want to know. And since many estate planning strategies—indeed, some of the most effective ones—require you to give up control of your assets during your lifetime, they seem downright scary. An irrevocable trust, for example, can't be undone. So why would anybody set one up? Because it can save a whole passel of estate taxes and protect your assets from any miscreant who decides to sue you simply because you have a lot of money.

Therefore, you may need to get over some of your fears about what may seem to you to be newfangled strategies, but which millions of people have used to minimize taxes and pass assets to loved ones. Just because you've never heard of them before doesn't mean there's something fishy about them. Still, you must watch out for those not-so-honest attorneys and life insurance representatives who may try to sell you products and services you don't need, or, worse, get you into defective instruments that fail to comply with the law.

Before considering any estate planning strategies, decide what's important to you and your family. Keep those goals uppermost in your mind as you navigate the estate planning waters so you won't be swayed by fast-talking "advisors" who try to sell you on multigenerational tax-saving strategies when all you really want to do is make sure your spouse is taken care of after you die. Never forget the human side of estate planning even as your calculator works overtime figuring out all the financial benefits.

CREDIT-SHELTER TRUST—FOR MARRIED COUPLES WITH OVER $650,000 IN ASSETS

The basic estate planning strategy mentioned earlier that allows both husband and wife to take full advantage of their respective $650,000 exemption equivalent is called a credit-shelter trust. You set it up so that when the first spouse dies, the amount that qualifies for the estate-tax exemption—$650,000 in 1999—goes into a trust instead of going directly to the surviving spouse. The surviving spouse gets the income from the trust as long as he or she is alive, while someone—usually a relative or professional advisor—manages the assets. Then when the surviving spouse dies, the assets in the trust, as well as any property owned by the surviving spouse, go to the children (if that's what you want). The assets from the credit-shelter trust are not taxed again. Only the surviving spouse's assets are subject to taxation.

With a credit-shelter trust, each spouse gets to shelter up to $650,000 from estate taxes, for a total of $1.3 million. Without it, only $650,000 would be sheltered upon the second spouse's death. And remember that the exemption equivalent increases to $1 million in 2006, enabling husbands and wives to pass a total of $2 million free of estate tax.

What's more, the appreciation on the assets held in the trust aren't subject to estate taxes. Let's say the second spouse lives another twenty years after the first spouse's death and the $650,000 grows to $2 million. The children will inherit the

$2 million estate-tax free (although they will have to pay capital gains taxes on the appreciation over $650,000 when they sell the assets).

In order for assets to pass to a credit-shelter trust, they must be held in each spouse's individual name (not joint). You do not need to place the assets in the trust right away. Rather, you can establish the trust with a *pour-over will* in which you designate which assets should go into the trust when you die.

LIVING TRUST—FOR PEOPLE
WHO WANT TO AVOID PROBATE

If you don't want your financial dealings to become a matter of public record by going through the probate process, you can set up a living trust and avoid all that publicity. By avoiding probate, you'll also be avoiding the administrative expenses and time delays—anywhere from six months to two years—during which your assets are tied up and unavailable to your heirs.

With a living trust—so named because it takes effect while you are living—you place your assets in trust and name you and your spouse as initial beneficiaries and trustees. You name your children (or whoever you want) as secondary beneficiaries. If you make the trust *revocable*, you have complete control over it. You can take income from it, sell trust assets and keep the proceeds, change the secondary beneficiaries, even cancel it entirely. Upon your death, the trust becomes irrevocable, which means nobody can change the terms of it. That's what you want. One of the benefits of a living trust is that it is more difficult to contest than a will. And because it doesn't go through probate, your assets can be distributed immediately to heirs, unless you specify some other arrangement. Revocable living trusts do not save estate taxes or income taxes. As the trust's initial beneficiary, you are responsible for paying income tax just as if the assets were held in your own name.

To avoid some of these tax liabilities, you can set up an *irrevocable* living trust. Irrevocable means just that—you can't undo the trust and you can't change the terms of it. You can't even add or delete beneficiaries. Assets transferred to an irrevocable trust cannot be taken back. In short, once you set it up, you give up control over the assets. But what you get in exchange are some pretty powerful tax benefits. Not income tax benefits, because the trust still has to pay income tax (unless the income is distributed to beneficiaries). But once assets are transferred to the trust, any future appreciation will not increase the size of your estate. So you can put up to $650,000 worth of assets into an irrevocable trust (the unified credit amount so there'll be no estate or gift tax), add $10,000 a year per beneficiary (the amount you can give away each year tax-free), and as the assets grow, the value of what used to be your estate grows without increasing your (or rather, your heirs') estate tax liability.

TESTAMENTARY TRUST—CONTROLLING YOUR ESTATE FROM THE GRAVE

Unlike living trusts, which take effect while you're still alive, testamentary trusts kick in after you die. Testamentary trusts allow you to be more specific about who should get your assets—and when. For example, if you have a spendthrift son, you may not want him to receive his inheritance until after he's finished with fast cars and extravagant living (age 30? 40?). A *qualified terminable interest property* (Q-Tip) *trust* allows you to provide income for your spouse for his or her lifetime, after which the assets are given to the beneficiaries *you* choose. This type of trust is commonly used to ensure that the children of the union inherit the money and not someone your spouse may later remarry. If you are on your second marriage, a Q-Tip trust will ensure that your assets go to the children of your first marriage.

LIFE INSURANCE TRUSTS—TO PROVIDE LIQUID FUNDS FOR ESTATE TAXES

If your estate consists largely of illiquid assets—real estate or a family business—you'll want to make sure your heirs have enough money to pay the estate taxes without having to sell the assets at what could be distressed prices. Life insurance is the perfect tool for this because it pays cash to beneficiaries income tax-free. And if the insurance is owned by an irrevocable trust (and not you), the proceeds will not be part of your estate and therefore be free of estate taxes as well. To save premium costs, you can purchase a *second-to-die* policy, which pays off after the second spouse dies.

CHARITABLE REMAINDER TRUSTS— FOR GIVING AND RECEIVING

A charitable remainder trust can be set up as a living trust or as a testamentary trust. As a living trust, it gives you an immediate tax deduction for your charitable contribution and also provides income for you and/or your family while the property is in trust. In the trust agreement, you can arrange for the charity to get the trust's assets at some future date, say at your death, or some number of years after your death. If you set it up as a testamentary trust, you can specify that the trust provide income to your beneficiary for life and that the remainder of the trust's assets go to a specified charity or institution at the beneficiary's death. This strategy, in addition to providing current income tax benefits and ongoing income, also reduces the value of your taxable estate while making the world a better place.

If these estate planning strategies sound simple and uncomplicated, it's because we have left out the myriad details that allow them to be customized for all different circumstances. This chapter is designed to serve as an overview of estate planning only—to introduce you to some of the techniques available to people who want to take care of their families while minimizing taxes. Because the laws are so complex (and changing all the time!), and because there are so many legal loopholes that really can save you money while ensuring that your wishes are carried out, we urge you to find a good estate planning attorney. But don't delay. The whole point of estate planning is to do it *before* it is needed.

CHAPTER SEVENTEEN

Family Planning

*Family: A unit composed not only of children,
but of men, women, an occasional animal,
and the common cold.*

—Ogden Nash

The great thing about family, according to Yogi Berra, is that when you have to go there, they have to take you in. Now, we know that one of the reasons you bought this book is so you could arrange your financial affairs so you would *not* be dependent on family. If you're like most people, you don't want to have to go there . . . and you probably don't want them to have to come to you. Financial independence is everyone's goal. To be able to take care of yourself with little or no outside help, and to have family members do the same, makes for strong family relations and prevents money issues from undermining the love and respect you naturally feel for one another.

Still, family is family. And money is such an important part of life that it's impossible to separate the two. Some people avoid family discussions about money because they're afraid it will strain family relations. But really, the opposite is true. When you lay everything out on the table, you have an opportunity to resolve questions and concerns that had been lying just below the surface and which, if not addressed, really could strain family relations. If you're worried that your aging parents may have to go into a nursing home, for example, you'll want to start preparing for it now. You'll want to know if they have enough assets to cover long-term care; if not, you may want to think about buying some insurance for them. If you don't talk about these things now, you could feel increasing stress and anxiety as a direct result of your concerns over Mom and Dad. Now, how good is that for family relations?

The keys to merging family and money are honesty and love. When you talk about finances with family members, do it in a loving way and make it clear that your motives are unselfish. Tell your parents that you want to know what they have so you can help them, not because you're thinking about your inheritance. Likewise, share your own financial information with your grown children so they can help you and also plan their own future. When you communicate with honesty and love, you can resolve uncomfortable situations without rancor. For example, if an adult child asks you for money that you don't want to give, explain truthfully and lovingly why you can't honor the request. Perhaps you're worried about your own retirement or you just want the child to have the experience of using his or her own resources. Reinforce your loving position by suggesting a compromise or offering alternative solutions for obtaining the money.

And start talking to your grandchildren about finances. Teach them how to handle money, and share some of the lessons you've learned about saving, investing, and smart spending. Think of age-appropriate games to play, from comparison-shopping lollipops to pretend stock-picking contests. It's too bad none of this is taught in school, because so many young people misuse credit while they're in college and find themselves totally clueless about financial management when they get out on their own. One of the most important legacies you can leave your children and grandchildren, in addition to any money you might leave them, is the sense to handle it wisely.

INTEGRATING FAMILY AND FINANCES

In addition to creating a general open environment in which family members are encouraged to talk about money, you'll want to do some specific things to ensure that everyone's best interests are addressed. One, you'll want to let at least one person in your family know what you have and where it is in case something happens to you. Two, you'll want to sign a durable power of attorney so your financial affairs can be handled without interruption should you become unable to handle them yourself. And three, you'll want to stay on top of family changes and adjust your plans accordingly. Each of these to-do items is discussed in the next sections.

MAKE A LIST

A website called "found money" (www.foundmoney.com) keeps track of unclaimed bank accounts that have been taken over by the state. You can enter someone's name and it will tell you if that person left money lying in a bank account somewhere. Why would anybody leave money in a bank account? It's usually because they died and never told anybody that the money was there. Don't do this to your loved ones. Make a list of everything you have and where it is. Keep the list in a safe place and tell at least one person in your family where the list can be found should *you* be found—shall we say, indisposed. Do not put the list in a safe deposit box because in some states safe deposit boxes are sealed at death, and there will be information on this list that you'll want your loved ones to have right away. Here's what to put on the list:

- Who's in charge
- Information about wills and trusts
- Assets and liabilities
- Important instructions

Who's in Charge

If something happens to you, somebody else will need to take over. If you become ill or incapacitated, you'll want a competent person to step in and handle your affairs. Not just health care decisions, as discussed in Chapter 15, but financial matters as well. You can arrange this by signing a durable power of attorney (discussed below). If the person named in your durable power of attorney is different from the loved one for whom you are leaving this list, indicate on the list the person named in the durable power of attorney and his or her phone number. Also, when you die, your executor will need to step in and settle your estate. On your list, indicate the name of your executor and his or her phone number. Also include on your list the names and telephone numbers of close relatives and important advisors, such as your attorney, accountant, stockbroker, and insurance agent.

Information About Wills and Trusts

The original copies of your will and/or trust may be held by your attorney or put in a safe deposit box. Your executor should have a photocopy of each document. On the list, indicate what legal instruments you have executed and who has copies of them.

Assets and Liabilities

List all of your bank and brokerage accounts with the name of the institution and account number. Better yet, photocopy a recent statement of each to assist in contacting the institution and locating the account. List any annuities and insurance policies you have, along with the phone numbers of the insurance companies. List pension information and phone numbers. List real estate holdings and tell where the deeds can be found. List personal property, like stamp or coin collections, and where they are located. Also list any loans you have outstanding, including the names of the institutions and account numbers.

Important Instructions

If you have children or elderly parents, indicate who should care for them temporarily in case the person you named as guardian in your will is not immediately available. If you have pets, tell how to care for them. If you're employed, leave the name and phone number of your employer. If you own a business, indicate what immediate steps should be taken until the executor takes over. Leave spare keys to the house and car and indicate on the list where the keys can be found. Write down any other important information, like medications you must have and where they are. Give funeral instructions or, if you have prepared a more elaborate burial plan, indicate where it is.

When drawing up your list, generally think about what your loved one would need to know and do should something happen to you and write it down.

EXECUTE A DURABLE POWER OF ATTORNEY

In Chapter 15 we talked about a health care power of attorney in which you name another person to make medical decisions for you in case you become too ill to do so. With a durable power of attorney for finances, you can authorize someone to step in and pay bills or direct the sale of assets in order to keep your financial affairs going. By the way, the word "durable" in durable power of attorney means that it stays in force even if you become incompetent (that's the whole idea), unlike a general power of attorney, which terminates when the signer becomes incompetent.

By signing a durable power of attorney while you are still healthy and of sound mind, you can avoid the possibility of your loved ones having to go through a lengthy court procedure to have you declared incompetent and having a conservator or guardian appointed to take over your affairs. With a durable power of attorney, you can name your own *attorney-in-fact*, choosing someone you trust to carry out your wishes. If you're worried that your attorney-in-fact might exercise his or her powers while you're still competent, you may be able to execute a *springing* power of attorney (available in some states), which does not take effect until you are deemed incompetent. However, it takes court action to have you declared incompetent, causing delays that might tie up your affairs. A better solution might be to let your loved one or attorney keep the durable power of attorney and call the attorney-in-fact if and when it is determined that it should be called into play.

The person you choose to handle your financial affairs need not be the same one directing your health care decisions. When choosing your *attorney-in-fact*, consider the person's business sense and how familiar he or she is with your situation. Also, of course, consider how much you trust that person to handle your money and to protect your family as you would.

If you have a living trust, you may not need a separate durable power of attorney. Trust documents usually specify a secondary trustee who is authorized to take over should the primary trustee (you) become unable to serve in that capacity.

KEEP UP WITH FAMILY CHANGES

Even though you're probably years—even decades—away from needing any of these estate planning arrangements, you'll feel great to have everything taken care of. With your durable power of attorney(s), you know your health care decisions and financial dealings will be handled. With your beneficiary designations and your wills, trusts, and other estate planning documents properly executed, you know that your property will go where you want it to after you die. With selected insurance policies in force, you know you are protected against the various catastrophes that might strike. What's left?

Even after all of these arrangements have been made, you still have to keep an eye on them—or, more accurately, your family—so you can update your estate plan as appropriate. Even though some wills contain standard language providing for the addition of any children or grandchildren born after the will is executed, it's best to review your entire estate plan whenever there's a birth, death, marriage, or divorce in your family. And you always should review your plan once a year or so in case the laws change or you change your mind about some of the decisions you made earlier.

COPING WITH CHANGE

Family dynamics are, well, dynamic. Most married couples would like to grow old together and die at the same time, but unfortunately it usually doesn't work out that way. When one spouse dies first, the other is left behind for some period of time. When married couples divorce, they both must pick up the emotional and financial pieces of their lives. When older people remarry, they must integrate their new spouse into the family plan in order to make sure children from the first marriage are taken care of. And then there are people who at some point in their lives decide to follow an unconventional lifestyle by eschewing marriage despite emotionally strong bonds to a partner; when this happens, they must work around pro-marriage laws to ensure that their wishes are carried out.

LOSS OF A SPOUSE

Most people would agree that losing a spouse to death is one of the most stressful experience a person can have. Without minimizing the emotional trauma caused by the sheer physical absence of the loved one, there's no doubt that a surviving spouse who is left well off financially and who is spared the trouble of making difficult decisions at a time of grief will have an easier time of it. That's why we urge you, if you are married, to get your affairs in order and to consider that the odds are pretty good that one of you will die first. Make as many joint decisions as you can now, so the surviving spouse will not have to make them alone later on. Involve your children in these decisions as much as possible, since they will be responsible for providing emotional support to the surviving spouse.

The most important advice we can give newly widowed people is to hold off on making any big, irrevocable decisions for at least a year. Don't sell the house and move. Don't put your money into any investments you don't fully understand and that you can't get out of without penalty. Don't remarry right away. Don't let anybody pressure you into anything. Tell them you are a grieving widow (or widower) and that you are not in your right mind because of your loss. And it's true. You may feel relatively okay after the initial mourning period is over, but an emotional trauma of this magnitude can cause your mind to play tricks on you. So take it easy.

The first thing you will need to do is locate all of your assets. If you and your spouse have been working together on the plans and strategies outlined in this book, you already know where things are and can carry on pretty much as before. If not, you may have some digging to do. Start by calling your spouse's advisors—attorney, accountant, stockbroker, insurance agent—and enlist their help in locating assets and transferring them into your own name. If you'll be receiving life insurance proceeds, you'll need to do something with the money. Again, we warn you not to do anything rash. Just put it into a money market fund until you feel comfortable investing it. Do not convert the insurance proceeds into a long-term contract that would prohibit you from getting at the money. You may need it.

If you have not yet started receiving Social Security benefits, call the Social Security Administration at 800-772-1213 or visit your local office to see what benefits you're entitled to. If you have children under 16, you can begin receiving benefits regardless of your age. If not, you may begin receiving benefits based on your spouse's work history at age 60. Once you turn 62 you can switch to your own work history if that would result in a higher benefit amount.

If your spouse was employed or receiving a corporate pension, contact the human resources department at your spouse's employer and report your spouse's death. Find out what your options are as surviving spouse, and check with your advisors or a trusted friend if you need help making decisions. If your spouse was a veteran, contact the Department of Veterans Affairs. It will reimburse you for some of the burial and funeral expenses as long as you file a claim within two years after your spouse's burial. You may also be eligible for a pension.

And finally, you'll want to update your estate plan and name new beneficiaries in wills, trusts, and IRAs.

DIVORCE

For some people, a divorce late in life after many years of marriage can be as traumatic as the death of a spouse. Unfortunately, our society doesn't have established ways of grieving for a spouse lost to divorce. You're expected to pick yourself up and carry on. You can't escape major decision-making after a divorce because there's property to divide and divorce terms to agree to. Even so, you may not be in the proper frame of mind to make long-lasting decisions. So be sure to get the help you need—a good attorney for the divorce negotiations and a group of friends for the emotional support.

Your attorney will tell you this, of course, but keep in mind that whatever assets you end up with after the divorce will have to last you the rest of your life. Unless you plan to go back to work (not a bad idea for sanity purposes), you'll be living off the income from your settlement, plus any Social Security you may be entitled to. By the way, you can collect Social Security based on your spouse's work history if you were married at least ten years, have been divorced for two years, and have not remarried. You may begin collecting benefits when both you and your ex-spouse reach age 62. Any benefits you collect as a divorced spouse will not affect your ex-spouse's benefits or any spousal benefits his or her new spouse may receive. If benefits based on your own work history would be higher, you can take the higher amount (and not worry about losing benefits if you remarry). If there's even a chance that divorce may be in your future, you should contact Social Security to find out what your benefits would be under your spouse's record vs. your own. You may want to boost your own benefits by earning as much income as possible between now and then.

Once the property has been divided and assets transferred into your own name, you will want to update your estate plan, adding or changing beneficiaries to wills, trusts, and IRAs.

REMARRIAGE

Remarriage is one of those happy family changes. There's nothing sweeter than an elderly couple becoming teenagers again when they decide to tie the knot and vow to spend the rest of their lives together. Of course, estate attorneys and financial book writers like us have to throw a cold dose of reality on the festivities and warn both spouses that if they don't make specific arrangements for their children from a prior marriage, these children will be left out in the cold when it comes to inheritance. The laws of succession in most states grant all or some of the deceased spouse's assets to the surviving spouse—unless overridden by a properly executed will or trust arrangement. What most remarrying people want is to have their surviving spouse taken care of for as long as he or she lives, after which the assets would go to the children from the first marriage. Since this is what each spouse wants—he wants his assets to go to his kids, she wants her assets to go to her kids—they will need to keep their property separate and use legal instruments to effect the transfer of property.

Some couples consider drawing up prenuptial agreements before marriage. While these documents are controversial among younger couples because they seem to undermine the whole till-death-do-us-part promise, they make a great deal of sense for older couples who need to keep their property separate for the benefit of succeeding generations. In lieu of a prenuptial agreement, some couples execute a postnuptial agreement accomplishing virtually the same thing. Drawing up the agreement after the marriage is a more romantic gesture because it does not make the marriage a condition of signing the document and demonstrates faith that you will be able to agree on the terms. Besides, you may already be married when it occurs to you that such an agreement may be in the best interests of your family.

UNCONVENTIONAL LIFESTYLES

At one time in our culture it was definitely frowned upon for two people to live together without benefit of marriage. It's more accepted now, especially among older couples who feel a strong commitment to one another but have chosen not to marry due to the legal entanglements such a union would create. Then there are the many kinds of committed relationships in which two people care deeply for each other but do not marry: same-sex couples who would marry if they could; siblings who live together and support each other in their old age;

friends who have adopted each other as soul mates. When the bonds of human relationships transcend the laws that dictate financial dealings, you must work around the laws and essentially create your own. The health care power of attorney, for example, offers a way for you to name the person you want to direct your medical care. Without it, a family member other than your significant other (a parent or adult child, for example) could take over. The estate planning tools discussed in Chapter 16 allow you to get around the laws of succession in your state and leave your assets to the person (people) you want. If you follow what is considered an unconventional lifestyle—at least as far as some of our antiquated laws are concerned—it's more important than ever that you take the law into your own hands and make sure your loved ones are provided for.

The purpose of this chapter on family planning is to recall and reinforce the whole reason you are doing financial planning in the first place: to protect and care for your family. With so many rules and regulations to keep track of concerning investments, taxes, insurance, and the like, it's easy to get distracted from the fundamental values that must infuse all of your financial dealings. As you go about implementing the various strategies suggested in this book, we urge you to place love of family and concern for others' well-being above all.

CHAPTER EIGHTEEN

Getting Going

One must change one's tactics every ten years
if one wishes to maintain one's superiority.

—Napoleon Bonaparte

Now that you have an understanding of what you must have, know, and do in order to secure a long and happy retirement, we hope you will take advantage of the motivation that led you to read this book in the first place to take the next step and get your financial affairs in order. If there were any chapters that you did not fully grasp in your first reading, please go back and review them. Our goal in writing this book was to pack as much useful information into it as possible. The downside of this, of course, is that there may have been too much information for some people to absorb in one pass. If you're feeling confused and overwhelmed at this point, go easy on yourself. Consider your first reading an introduction to the material, and keep the book handy so you can refer to it later.

PULLING EVERYTHING TOGETHER

The most important action you can take at this point is to make sure you know what you have and where everything is. If your record-keeping system is less than ideal—that is, if you can't immediately put your hands on a file that lists all of your assets and where they are located—get started now pulling together account statements and other documents and organizing a filing system that works for you and your family. Make it is easy to maintain, so as new statements come in the mail, you'll know exactly where to put them and will have no need to let papers pile up until you get around to filing them.

If, while you were reading this book, you came across items needing attention, make a list of those items and start taking care of them. For example, if you are over 55 and haven't started receiving Social Security yet, call the Social Security Administration at 800-772-1213 and ask for a Personal Earnings and Benefit Statement so you can verify your earnings record. If the chapter on insurance reminded you that you need to update your policies, put that on your to-do list as well. And, of course, if you do not have a will, make an appointment to talk to an estate planning attorney so you can get that taken care of as soon as possible.

PERFORMING
ROUTINE MAINTENANCE

Once you have pulled your papers together and completed everything on your to-do list, you'll want to stay on top of things to make sure nothing slips between the cracks or gets out of hand. Routine maintenance is just as important for financial matters as it is for your car, your teeth, your house, and your body. Set up a schedule to review your financial dealings no less than once each quarter. Go over your investment accounts, your insurance policies, your estate plan (any new grandchildren?); verify that all of these areas are functioning as they should; and make any minor adjustments that may be necessary.

STAYING FLEXIBLE
IN THE FACE OF CHANGE

The rate at which our world is changing is truly mind-boggling. And what is unique about some of the major changes that are occurring is that they have been nearly impossible to predict. Who could have imagined, for example, that the Internet would revolutionize so many people's lives in so many different ways. (If you haven't embraced the Internet yet, just wait!) So you can't assume that the knowledge you used to put your financial plan in place won't undergo revision next week or next year. (We're keeping our fingers crossed as we write this book that the information will still be valid by the time you read it!) Tax laws change. Social Security and Medicare probably will undergo major revisions in the near future. The financial markets—impossible to predict anyway—could start doing crazy things. Who knows what changes are lurking around the next bend?

The only thing you can do about this dizzying pace of change is accept new developments as they occur and make adjustments as necessary. The worst thing you can do is cling to old assumptions even as new evidence is staring you in the face. By going with the flow, you can ride the tide wherever it takes you, and by keeping a positive attitude, you are sure to end up in a better place.

We hope you have gotten something out of this book that will stay with you as you go about planning your financial future, and we wish you and your family good fortune and a long and happy life.

Index